WHEN THERAPY GOES WRONG

LEARNING FROM CHALLENGES AND IMPROVING PRACTICE

SATINDER PANESAR

Published in 2025 by Discover Your Bounce Publishing

www.discoveryourbouncepublishing.com

ISBN: 978-1-914428-33-3

Although the author and publisher have made every effort to ensure that the information in this book is correct at the time of going to print, the author and publisher do not assume and therefore disclaim liability to any party. The author and the publisher will not be held responsible for any loss or damage save for that caused by their negligence.

Although the author and the publisher have made every reasonable attempt to achieve accuracy in the content of this book, they assume no responsibility for errors or omissions.

Page design and typesetting by
Discover Your Bounce Publishing

DEDICATION

To my granddaughter, Nyah Panesar, whose inspiration and light remind me of the importance of purpose and perseverance. You are my "why," and this book is a testament to the legacy I hope to leave for you.

CONTENTS

ACKNOWLEDGEMENTS

Thank you to you, the authors that have contributed to this book. When I reached out to you for collaboration, there was no hesitation at all. I deeply appreciate your passion, energy and you for trusting me to share your experiences; your openness has made this book possible. Thank you to the therapists (supervisees) I have had the privilege of working with, past and present: I cherish the work we have done together. I know my style is unique, but its success lies in the meaningful connections we've established. You've certainly kept me on my toes and I continue to learn and grow because of you.

To all the clients I have worked with over the past 30 years: Your journeys have been my inspiration. I remain as passionate about this work today as I was when I first began. You have shaped me into the therapist I am today. Through all the ups and downs and many side steps I've taken, your journeys have taught me invaluable lessons.

A heartfelt thank you to Nicky Marshall of Discover Your Bounce Publishing: Your prompt communication, steadfast support, authenticity, and genuine love for this book have meant the world to me.

Appreciation Also Goes To...

I would like to extend my heartfelt gratitude to Pat Slattery for the unwavering confidence he has instilled in me as both my Coach and Mentor. Your guidance came into my life at precisely the right moment, providing clarity and inspiration when I needed it most. Thank you for your kindness, your belief in my potential, and the invaluable introductions to your extensive network. Your support has been pivotal in my journey, and I am deeply appreciative of the impact you have made.

Thank you to Alison Carter and Laurence Herbert, who have been alongside me from the beginning. They have both encouraged me and held the most crucial safe space for me when I needed it the most, it's been invaluable.

Thank you to Vicky Palmer, for your presence, belief, wisdom and joy! Your support has been a source of strength.

There are so many more individuals I would like to thank. While it's impossible to name every single person, but to those of you who I've spoken to about this book - you know who you are - thank you!

I want to express my gratitude to Paul McFadden and the Elite Mastermind community. The support, collaboration, and inspiration from the Elite Mastermind community have been nothing short of incredible. Thank you all for being part of this journey!

BIOGRAPHY

Satinder Panesar's academic journey began at the University of Derby, where she earned her Master's degree before pursuing a Supervisor's Qualification at Strathclyde University. This educational foundation set the stage for her to become a distinguished Psychotherapist, Clinical Supervisor, and Consultant in the field of mental health.

Satinder's journey in the field of mental health is adorned with recognition and accreditation. A registered and accredited member of the British Association for Counselling & Psychotherapy (BACP) and the National Counselling & Psychotherapy Society (NCPS), Satinder's affiliations serve as a testament to her unwavering commitment to the highest standards of professional and ethical practice.

Satinder is a member of the BACP Healthcare Executive Division for the four nations - the aim is to promote and support excellence in healthcare counselling/psychotherapy & supervision.

As an Integrative Psychotherapist, Satinder's expertise spans over 25 years and encompasses diverse sectors. She has made significant contributions in the Third sector, the NHS Greater Glasgow & Clyde, and the private sector. Her ability to deliver face-to-face and remote counselling, both within the UK & Globally, speaks to her adaptability and unwavering dedication to making mental health accessible to all, transcending borders and cultures.

An advocate for holistic growth, Satinder extends her expertise beyond individual sessions. As a Trainer, she imparts her wisdom in a variety of environments, shedding light on an array of topics. Her transformative influence resonates not only within the walls of her office but also in classrooms, boardrooms, and beyond.

Satinder's impact continues to amplify as an Individual/Group Clinical Supervisor, where she provides invaluable guidance and support to fellow mental health professionals. Furthermore, as a Reflective Practice Facilitator, she empowers individuals and teams to navigate the complexities of their professional journeys in non- clinical settings, e.g Higher Education, Work Coaches, Legal Professionals, Politicians, Entertainment, Arts & Theatre and Homelessness and Housing.

Satinder's contributions are further enhanced by her role in Coaching, Mentoring, and Clinical Consultancy.

However, it is perhaps in her unique cultural proficiency that Satinder truly shines. Fluent in Punjabi, she navigates conversations with a deep understanding of tradition and culture. This exceptional ability allows her to forge connections, offer guidance and provide not only specialist therapy to clients but also culturally sensitive Clinical Supervision to therapists that resonates on a profound level. She bridges cultural gaps within small communities and understands the nuances of tradition and trauma that shape individuals' experiences. This unique perspective enables her to address issues that arise in small communities, ultimately contributing to healing on a profound level.

Satinder Panesar's journey is a reminder that every interaction in therapy is a step towards growth and personal learning. Her work, her experience, and her passion come together to create a mosaic of understanding, compassion, and transformation.

Purpose

Therapy has always been portrayed as a transformative process; a sanctuary where individuals seek solace, healing, and personal growth. It's a field that thrives on empathy, compassion, and a deep belief in the human capacity for change. However, in my own journey as a therapist, I have encountered moments when therapy took an unexpected turn. Despite my best intentions, the path veered off course, and the outcomes fell short of both my clients' expectations and my own. These experiences have been humbling and deeply reflective, reminding me that even in a field dedicated to healing, we are all human and fallible.

This book is a reflection on those experiences. This is how the story began...

It all started with a conversation with a therapist, that made me smile. He remarked, "You are so experienced, I bet you have never got therapy wrong." I responded by acknowledging we are all human, and no matter how qualified or experienced one is, there is always a possibility of getting it wrong.

This conversation sparked an idea for this book. I began reflecting on my own experiences of 'getting it wrong' and discussed these reflections with my clinical supervisor. As a clinical supervisor myself, I often hear similar reflections from my supervisees. Clinical supervision is a safe space to share these experiences in confidence. Many of my past and present supervisees will have heard my mantra:

"Bring to supervision what you don't want to bring."

And they certainly did! It was then I thought a collaborative piece on this topic would be invaluable. The response to my call for contributions was incredible, and I had to limit the number of chapters. I chose 13, a number I consider lucky. Perhaps there will be a follow-up - watch this space!

As you read through the chapters, you will witness the uniqueness of each writer's experience shining through. The diversity in their styles of writing reflects their individuality and personal perspectives, which was precisely what I envisioned for this book. Each chapter carries its own voice and method of presentation, making every contribution distinctive and authentic. I intentionally embraced these differences, as they enrich the narrative and offer readers a multifaceted journey through the collective wisdom and experiences shared in these pages. Each contributor has their contact details at the back of the book so you can connect further.

The variety is truly phenomenal, showcasing that therapy can go wrong at any point in time.

This book is a testament to the importance of reflecting on and learning from these moments.

INTRODUCTION

In recounting the stories of individuals who have faced disappointment or dissatisfaction within the therapeutic setting, my intention is not to undermine the importance of therapy itself. Rather, it is a call to critically examine the factors that can contribute to adverse experiences, be they systemic, ethical, interpersonal, or otherwise. By doing so, we can work towards enhancing the therapeutic experience and fostering a safer, more effective environment for all.

I must acknowledge the bravery of those who have graciously shared their personal stories of therapy that fell short of their expectations. Their narratives serve as important reminders that therapy, like any human endeavour, is not infallible. Their voices deserve to be heard and their experiences acknowledged, for it is through their courage that we can learn, grow, and strive for better outcomes in the future.

Additionally, I want to highlight the immense knowledge, dedication, and expertise that therapists bring to their work. The therapeutic field encompasses a wide array of modalities, each grounded in years of research, practice, and a genuine commitment to helping others heal and grow. From cognitive-behavioural therapy, person centred, integrative practice to psychodynamic approaches, somatic practices, and beyond, therapists tailor their interventions to meet the unique needs of each individual. This diversity reflects the richness of the profession and the profound impact it has on countless lives.

To my fellow therapists, clinicians and mental health professionals, I invite you to approach this exploration with an open mind and a willingness to engage in introspection. By examining the narratives of when therapy went wrong, we can challenge our assumptions, enhance our practices, and foster a culture of continuous improvement within our field.

Lastly, I extend my gratitude to all that have embarked on this challenging journey with me. It is through your engagement and willingness to confront the complexities of therapy that we can collectively contribute to a safer, more ethical, and more effective therapeutic landscape. Together, let us navigate the difficult terrain when therapy goes wrong, holding space for introspection, growth, and a commitment to creating excellent experiences both for the therapist and the client.

To preserve the anonymity of the clients in this book, extensive measures have been taken to protect confidentiality; names, jobs, and other details such as locations and family make up have been changed. In some instances, multiple case stories have been integrated where there are similarities, weaving the experiences of several individuals into a single narrative. While many of these situations may seem familiar and may parallel your own experiences speaking loudly to you, rest assured that they have been carefully anonymised.

These accounts are shared with the sole purpose of learning from challenges and improving practice. They serve as a reminder that even in our most challenging moments, there are valuable lessons to be learnt.

Why read this book

This book is intended for a diverse audience with an interest in psychology, mental health, and the therapeutic process. It aims to appeal to multiple readerships, including:

Clients and therapy seekers: Those individuals who have personally experienced instances where therapy did not meet their needs or expectations. It offers validation, support, and insights that can help them process their own experiences and make more informed decisions about their therapeutic journey.

Mental health professionals: Therapists, counsellors, psychologists, and other mental health practitioners can benefit from this book by gaining a deeper understanding of the complexities and challenges that can arise within therapy. It encourages self-reflection, critical analysis, and the identification of potential pitfalls, ultimately fostering an environment for improved client care.

Students and researchers: Aspiring therapists and researchers in the field of mental health can gain valuable insights from the narratives shared in this book. It serves as a thought-provoking resource, offering real-world examples that highlight the importance of ethical considerations, professional development, and ongoing exploration within the field of psychotherapy. For students in particular at the start of the their clinical journey the importance of finding the right clinical supervisor is paramount.

Educators and supervisors: Those involved in training future therapists or providing supervision to practicing clinicians can utilise this book as a tool for stimulating discussions, case analysis, and ethical exploration. It prompts thoughtful conversations about the challenges and responsibilities inherent in the therapeutic process. I'd extend the invitation to Educators of emphasising the importance and meaning around accessing clinical supervision which is covered extensively.

General readers with an interest in counselling & psychotherapy: This book may also appeal to a broader audience curious about the dynamics of therapy and the human experience. It provides a unique perspective on the complexities and potential pitfalls of therapy, inviting readers to reflect on their own assumptions and beliefs about the therapeutic process.

By encompassing a range of perspectives, this book seeks to foster dialogue and empathy towards the therapeutic journey. It is a resource for those seeking a deeper understanding of the nuances and complexities of therapy, with the ultimate aim of contributing to a more informed and ethical therapeutic landscape.

I hope my journey is a reminder that every interaction in therapy is a step towards growth and personal learning. That my work, my experience, and my passion come together to create a mosaic of understanding, compassion, and transformation.

CHAPTER ONE

Empowering Self Determination:
The Importance of Cultural Humility

Ruth Daly

Ruth Daly is a clinical sexologist and psychotherapist with extensive experience in Gender, Sex, and Relationship Diversity (GSRD), neurodivergence, and trauma. Based in Greater Glasgow, Ruth offers in-person and remote therapy services across the UK, providing support for individuals, couples, polycules, and groups.

Driven by a passion for inclusivity and empowerment, Ruth specialises in creating safe, affirming spaces for all clients. Ruth is a member of the British Association for Counselling and Psychotherapy (BACP), the College of Sexual and Relationship Therapists (CORST), and Pink Therapy. Their approach is rooted in empathy, respect, and a deep understanding of diverse human experiences.

***

I have been actively involved in the field of GSRD for a significant period of time. It is an area that deeply resonates with my professional interests and personal dedication. GSRD, is a term created by Pink Therapy to broaden the scope of inclusivity and encourage open dialogue about the diverse experiences of individuals within the intricate realms of identity, sexuality, and interpersonal connections (Davies 2021). GSRD aims to create greater awareness and recognition for marginalised communities beyond the traditional LGBT spectrum. Within the GSRD framework, the concept of gender encompasses individuals who identify with traditional binary notions of gender, those who embrace a more fluid understanding, as well as those who do not associate with any particular gender at all.

Sex is taken to cover multiple meanings including sexuality, sexual orientation and the act of sex itself, but also biological sex in order to be inclusive of intersex persons who do not fit the typical binary definitions of male and female bodies. Relationship Diversity in this context emphasises the vast array of possibilities in terms of how individuals form connections with each other. Often a relationship is assumed to be heterosexual and monogamous, GSRD embraces the inclusion of individuals who identify as aromantic, or asexual, engage in BDSM (Bondage, Discipline or Domination), sadism (or submission), masochism practices, practice celibacy, or adopt ethical non-monogamy (Davies, Neves 2023). By adopting this framework, I strive to foster a more inclusive and understanding environment that acknowledges and respects the various experiences and identities within our society.

In the early stages of my career, I was eager to adhere strictly to my training. This approach stemmed from my belief that strict adherence to these principles would guarantee utmost client satisfaction and enable me to excel. Although this dedication still holds true, I have since recognised I needed to incorporate more elements to influence my approach when working with clients. During my initial training, the concept of gender was touched on very minimally, yet it still surpasses the standard level of training typically offered. The training I received emphasised guiding clients towards consulting their GP to explore transitioning as the default. At the time, this approach seemed logical to me, considering the lengthy waiting lists for treatment. I believed it was better to be proactive and place our clients on these lists as early as possible. It remains the case that Scottish law requires a medical diagnosis and evidence of having lived for two years in their acquired gender before an individual can 'legally' transition. Considering all these factors, I felt that my approach was supportive and constructive. However, I now recognise that although I personally have had positive experiences with my GP I had not considered how my privileges influenced those experiences. Consequently, I encouraged my clients to pursue a medical transition without fully considering the pressure this may create or the diverse social struggles they may face. Every client's journey is unique, and it is crucial to respect and acknowledge their individual circumstances and the factors that shape their identities.

Tracey was the client who sparked my realisation and need to improve. At the time of our initial session, she was 39 years old and primarily went by the name Terry, only sharing her true identity with a select few close friends. Tracey sought me out due to the distress she experienced from living a seemingly dual existence. During our first session, I inquired if she had consulted with her GP and upon learning she had not, I urged her to do so. I explained it is easier to remove herself from a waiting list than to reflect upon the time wasted not being on it. Tracey expressed her concerns to me, and I assured her that medical professionals maintain impartiality and solely desire what is best for her. Together, we dedicated an entire session to exploring what she could anticipate when broaching the topic of transitioning with her GP. Furthermore, we devised a comprehensive list of questions for her to ask at the appointment. When I inquired about her feelings regarding the upcoming GP appointment, Tracey admitted to a mix of nervousness and readiness, emphasising her desire to avoid any unnecessary delays. Following the appointment, witnessing Tracey's heartbreak and anguish as she detailed this encounter within the therapy room was both palpable and profound. The GP's words deeply wounded her, as their position of authority seemingly transformed their hurtful statement into an inescapable truth for Tracey. Although I initially felt anger towards the GP and wanted the blame to sit with them, I recognise and take accountability that I played a role in initiating this situation. If we had dedicated more time to helping Tracey build her self-confidence until she was in a place where she felt able to claim her gender, the outcome might have been different. This realisation prompted me to research the experiences of other transgender individuals during similar appointments and how they ensure their safety. I have since incorporated this knowledge into my professional practice. While I still believe it is important for individuals to communicate with their GPs, I will exercise caution when offering encouragement in such situations and strive for neutrality until the client is ready.

Three key takeaways from this experience

1. **Reflecting on bias and privilege:** Taking time to reflect upon your own biases and privileges is crucial, encompassing both the acknowledgement of their existence and the understanding of their impacts on your life and view of the world. Taking accountability for mistakes and learning from them is crucial to personal and professional growth. It is to continuously challenge yourself around the concept of your own shame when we end up getting it wrong. It was necessary to explore and understand the underlying purpose of my shame and evaluate whether it ultimately benefits anyone in the long run. A recognition that making mistakes is inevitable, it doesn't make you a bad therapist - only human. The measure of a good therapist is what you do after a mistake.

2. **Client-led approach:** I'm not sure I believe in full neutrality within a therapy room, it's a lot to ask of a therapist to go in as an empty vessel or metaphorical blank slate when we too live in this world and have our own experiences and opinions and sometimes, we inhabit the same community as our clients. Nonetheless, I strongly believe that it is our responsibility to openly acknowledge our biases with ourselves and our clients. Then strive to create an environment that allows us to be as impartial as possible. To achieve this, I actively engage in supervision and self-reflection, both of which help me navigate the delicate process of maintaining a balance while supporting my clients in their exploration.

3. **Continuous learning and cultural humility:** Legitimacy stress is a significant nuance of minority stress. Minority stress incorporates a broader sense of burden and stress due

to an individual's race, ethnicity, sexual orientation, and/ or gender identity. These struggles can extend beyond specific situations and become a fundamental part of an individual's daily life. Gender legitimacy stress is being confronted by the awareness that parts of society, some that the client may want to inhabit, regard their gender as being less 'real' than others or due to a mental illness that the client is delusional too. This not only devalues and stigmatises the client's gender, but also undermines the person';s authentic identity by labelling it as a mere 'fantasy' that can never be achieved - leading many, including the client, to believe they are inherently flawed. Consequently, such experiences heavily impact an individual's sense of belonging, self-worth, and personal safety. They may question whether it is safe to express their gender through clothing on certain streets, carefully consider the potential repercussions of using specific restrooms, and experience the pain of being misgendered by close friends and family or even colleagues, as well as the broader public. These constant reminders, reinforcing that the client is not seen and may never be truly recognised for their genuine self, contribute to the distressing nature of legitimacy stress.

How did this experience help you improve your practice?

This experience highlighted the need for a more client-centred impartial approach in therapy. Their voice and experience are always centred, this shift has allowed my clients to develop greater confidence and self-esteem. Moving away from a narrow focus on medical transition pathways to exploring a broader range of gender, sex and relationship diversity has allowed for more inclusive and empowering client interactions. It is important to envision yourself, alongside clients at a crossroads instead of a singular path, with no rush to make a choice providing support for as long as they require and enabling them to carve their own path forward, guided by their own unique needs and truths. Providing individuals with the opportunity to make their own choices not only fosters a sense of trust and confidence in themselves but can also contribute to a feeling of pride, acceptance and inclusivity.

It is essential to emphasise the significance of incorporating psychoeducation as an integral component of creating a supportive environment before making any decisions. This approach ensures my practice operates ethically, as informed consent serves as a foundation for all interventions. It is crucial that individuals have the opportunity to comprehend all available possibilities before selecting the best course of action for themselves. This aspect is instrumental in establishing trust and respect within my practice. Moreover, engaging in such conversations enables clients to become curious, ask questions and explore alternative perspectives, fostering valuable therapeutic work.

A tool I have discovered, and love is *The Trans Compass*, an innovative tool created by Ellis Morgan to enhance the efficacy of trans affirmation therapy, particularly for those contemplating or undergoing gender transition (Morgan 2023). This resource emphasises the significance of addressing gender legitimacy stress with a knowledgeable and inclusive outlook on the challenges commonly encountered by individuals in the community. It recognises how these experiences can impact a client's self-understanding and their ability to be understood by others. The use of the term trans in the title of the tool is being used most inclusively. Morgan is using trans as an umbrella term to highlight and hold all who experience a sense of queer gender differences as opposed to their cisgender counterparts. The tool is broken down into two fundamental aspects of gender transition. The first is a personal claim on a gender: 'Gender Claimed to Gender not Claimed' creating the north-south axis on the compass. This denotes a process of confidently embracing a distinct gender identity and asserting the right to claim it as one's own. This is held on a spectrum, as some can easily navigate their incongruence without too much deliberation and with a sense of confidence, while others can spend a long time in uncertainty.

The second is where an individual positions their transness in terms of their identity, as once someone has accepted there is a discrepancy in their gender identity, trans becomes part of their identity and it is up to that individual where they will sit on this spectrum, hence 'Trans Background to Trans Foreground' creating the east-west axis. Some individuals view their transgender identity solely from a biological standpoint, some who prefer not to identify or associate with being transgender, and others who consider it an integral part of their identity. When these two axes intersect, they form a simple four-quadrant diagram that can be used to explore intricate and nuanced discussions. Morgan has explicitly stated that this tool has been streamlined in order to enable a more inclusive conversation, thereby enabling individuals to ascertain the areas they resonate with most. Additionally, it is crucial for us to acknowledge that someone's identity and connection to that identity can evolve over time and it's important we hold space for that movement with clients.

I have expanded my lens of diversity to be more inclusive of heteronormativity, which some might argue is counterintuitive. Heteronormativity is typically understood as a representation of what is 'standard', therefore, the opposite of diversity. The argument being that heteronormativity is representative of what is assumed to be 'natural,' and creates a lot of privilege for those that fall within this categorisation (Hertzmann, Newbigin 2019). I have two reasons for adopting a more expansive lens: firstly, reducing the division between what is assumed as normative and what is othered but also secondly, to leave space for clients who take joy in having their transness more in the background. A client who highlighted this for me the most was Lewis he is 19 years old and began his transition at the age of 16. For him being trans is a small part of his story. He holds no shame but does like to keep it private. He stated that he does not care who around him is cis-gender and who is not, it is not his business, and his gender is no concern of others. He has expressed that he does not want to engage with the trans community directly. Not because he rejects it, but because he has other higher priorities in his life. From the outside his life appears to conform to typical expectations around the 'heteronormative' which carries a certain level of privilege he is aware of. I began working with him at the age of 16, he had already come out to his parents who then approached me to help support their son. During my time working with him, I felt jarred by his dismissal of the trans community, thinking there was underlying shame in him wanting to isolate himself. However, I was viewing his journey through a narrowed lens of how I thought queerness should be and it was my job to expand my narrative. By all means, explore shame or anything you feel as a practitioner might be underlying as well as giving resources. However, if you complete this work and don't find anything it does not mean you dig deeper. It means we allow the client to be the lead on their story, to accept their truth and narrative of how they want to be in their world.

If I had the opportunity to go back in time and give my past self the learning I have now, my process would be slowed down. I want to take a moment to recognise the difficulty involved when holding a slow process while working within a session limited organisation. During these instances, I prioritise utilising the time available to effectively empower the client with the necessary skills and resources for independently navigating their way forward, rather than solely focusing on reaching a predetermined goal. Additionally, being honest with myself and the client about what is achievable within our time together is necessary for informed consent. Rather than hastening the process, my intention would be to create an environment that promotes self-discovery and personal growth. I would prioritise acknowledging and respecting the client's individual journey and preferences, valuing their autonomy, and empowering them in making informed decisions. By placing the client's story at the forefront, my approach would involve a genuine curiosity about their experiences and aspirations for a fulfilling life.

How did clinical supervision support you through the experience?

Supervision was key for me in exploring and challenging my unconscious bias. It was so important that my supervisor understood the field I was working in considering the diversity within the context of GSRD. It is important to acknowledge the impossibility of knowing everything from all points of view. A skilled supervisor, through their guidance and encouragement, can assist in shedding light on areas where my awareness may be lacking. Thereby fostering personal growth and development. Coming to terms with my limitations was challenging. I previously saw this as a failure and that if I acknowledged my limits then I was validating my worst fear: that I would never be good enough as a practitioner. Supervision helped me to reframe this idea by reminding me of the core principles of GSRD, one of which is balancing cultural humility with cultural competency. This core principle helped to reduce my shame around 'getting it wrong.' Cultural competence is an ongoing commitment to learn, understand and appreciate the diverse behaviours, beliefs, language, values, and customs of distinct groups. By gaining this knowledge, we can more effectively relate and engage with clients from various racial, ethnic, socioeconomic, religious, and social backgrounds. Cultural humility involves recognising the complexities of identity, even for those with shared characteristics and backgrounds, we need to hold space for differences. It is a process of introspection and self-evaluation while maintaining a willingness to learn from others. Cultural humility means acknowledging that a clinician will never be fully competent regarding the multifaceted nature of our client's experiences. To cultivate cultural humility, it is crucial to engage in continuous learning and to go beyond conventional educational resources, such as textbooks. We should actively seek knowledge from the communities we serve, as well as from media, podcasts, and other sources. By adopting this approach, we can strive to improve our cultural competence to help meet the specific needs of our clients (Loue 2022). Here are some questions I have found helpful to reflect on to gain insight:

- Which aspects of my identity am I consciously aware of? Which do I value most and what is the underlying reason for that?
- Which parts of my identity could be considered privileged and/or marginalised?
- How might my sense of identity shift depending on the environment and situation?
- In others' perceptions, what aspects of my identity do they tend to emphasise?
- Which aspects are positively received, and by whom?
- What personal biases or blind spots might I have? How have my past experiences influenced the development of these biases?

What insights have you gained from being curious about the experience and from the process of self-reflection?

The process of creating an internal space for reflection without judgement has taken dedication, practice, and many tears. However, I firmly believe it is essential for the development of my skills, effectiveness, and intuition. In many ways, I compare it to a chef tasting their creation at each stage, even if they have followed the same recipe numerous times before. By engaging in self-reflection, I actively invite change into my practice. In the early stages of my career, the notion of change was unsettling and potentially unpredictable, causing fear. However, I learnt to overcome being stuck by this fear, recognising my goal is not to be completely fearless of change, but rather to be confident in my ability to handle change while still experiencing worry, trusting in my skills, experience, peers, supervisors and innately my own intuition. I have discovered that, personally, I find writing to be the most effective method for self-reflection. When I put my thoughts down on paper, I am able to examine them from a more objective standpoint, avoiding the potential echo chamber my head can create if I debate myself internally. I have curated a set of questions I choose from to explore the effectiveness of a session or intervention. These questions assist me in evaluating various aspects of a situation and help me consider if I have any blind spots. Once I have taken time to sit with and contemplate these questions, I discuss them during supervision to safeguard against any personal biases.

- What preconceived notions or assumptions influenced my decision to select this intervention? How did I come about those assumptions?
- Did I demonstrate a respectful attitude towards the client's autonomy and decision-making abilities? Can I evidence this?
- Did I maintain respect for the client's values, beliefs, and perspectives, even if they differ from my own? How did I show this?
- What emotions did I experience throughout the session or intervention?
- What knowledge and theories supported the decisions I made in working with this client?
- Who stands to benefit from this intervention, and is that benefit evident to the client?

What guidance and learning would you offer other professionals?

I acknowledge that while this guidance may appear straightforward in theory, implementing it can turn out to be more intricate than anticipated. It is crucial to acknowledge these abilities as valuable skills and to avoid feeling discouraged if our progress in them is not rapid.

Building a strong foundation takes time. I also want to respect that as practitioners, we all have our unique approaches and methods. Therefore, when I offer guidance, it is not meant to impose a uniform practice for everyone. Instead, I hope to facilitate nuanced discussions that each individual can internalise and adapt according to their own personal style.

- **Embrace change and vulnerability:** Allow space for your practice to change, the world around us is constantly evolving, therefore so too does our practice need to evolve. Change comes from a deep place of vulnerability which means it takes bravery to adapt. It's not a failing to admit we need to change, it's a failing to not evolve to help those who trust in us.

- **Introspection and re-evaluation:** Make it a priority to dedicate time for introspection and re-evaluation of the beliefs and principles that you hold as solid, immovable and fixed in your life, your community and within your view of humanity in your personal life, community, and overall understanding of humanity. Take into account not only the reasons behind the significance of these values in your present circumstances but also reflect upon the events and experiences that have contributed to the development of such a steadfast attachment to them. Additionally, ask yourself what would happen to your world if these shifted.

- **Client narrative and continuous learning:** To affirm a client's identity we need to understand their world and how they relate to and navigate it. This means embracing your client's narrative and being genuinely curious about their story. However, it is essential to maintain a delicate balance between acknowledging a client's unique experiences and burdening them with the responsibility of educating you about their community. While we can always learn from our clients, it is never appropriate to expect them to serve as our educators. Therefore, it is crucial to continuously enhance our knowledge and proficiency not only through traditional avenues such as textbooks, conferences, and professional development events, but also by actively engaging with the community itself, whether through podcasts, books, or participation in activism campaigns.

References

A - Dominic Davies (2021). What does GSRD mean? [online]. Pink Therapy. Available from: <https://pinktherapy.org/wp-content/uploads/2021/01/What-does-GSRD-mean-.pdf>.
[Accessed 25/09/2023].

B -Dominic Davies, Silva Neves (eds). (2023). Erotically Queer A Pink Therapy Guide for Practitioners. UK: Taylor.

C - Ellis Morgan (2023). The Trans Compass. In: Silva Neves and Dominic Davies, (ed). Relationally Queer, UK: Routledge

D - Leezah Hertzmann, Juliet Newbigin (eds). (2019). Sexuality and Gender Now: Moving Beyond Heteronormativity (Tavistock Clinic Series). UK: Routledge.

E - Sana Loue (2022). Diversity, Cultural Humility, and the Helping Professions: Building Bridges Across Difference. 1st. ed. New York: Springer.

Chapter Two

Freeing the Wounded Healer: A Mixture of Dread, Stuckness & Accountability

Annie Lee Garrigan

I was born into a first generation, immigrant family in a small town in Scotland during the 1970s. My working career began in research and consultancy in London, and East and Southeast Asia. I often thought about what I enjoyed most in my work, and it was always the helping part. I noticed how professionals would often talk about their personal challenges and when working in a shop, people would come in solely for a little human interaction, and even refuge. When I returned to study, I was instantly drawn to the helping profession. As a final year MSc. student at Abertay University, I was nominated for the Sarah Fletcher Prize for showing commitment to going above and beyond the expectations of the counselling degree and ever since, I have continued to foster the growth of my own unique way of helping. I have also begun to integrate into my work, aspects of my passion for creative arts, nature and tai chi. Since 2019, I have been a pluralistic counsellor in the further education sector and in private practice, alongside well-being projects with social enterprises. My current research interests are in somatic healing, neurodiversity, and social justice counselling.

Thinking back to my student days, I had attended a lecture on the qualities of effective therapists. There was strong evidence from research on brief outcome measures highlighting some therapists being more effective than others, over the assumption that the right therapy or interventions were being used. Based on my experiences in practice, I believe that to be true. I measure therapy going well, for instance, as when I helped clients achieve their goal, having an authentic relationship with them, client feedback forms showing positive evaluations and improved Core-OM results and clients referring other clients. CORE-OM (Clinical Outcomes in Routine Evaluation – Outcome Measure) is a widely used psychological assessment tool designed to evaluate the effectiveness of therapy by capturing changes in a client's mental health over time. Available in its full 34-item form (CORE-OM 34) or a shorter 10-item version (CORE-OM 10), it assesses four domains: well-being, problems, functioning, and risk, allowing clinicians to gauge distress levels and therapeutic progress. The pluralistic approach of collaborating, meta-communicating and working with client preferences created a steady holding for me and the rest was down to me to develop effectiveness as a therapist. Being mindful of the challenges of identifying as a wounded healer, I am sharing a personal account of what I learnt from exploring when 'my' therapy goes wrong. I hope this will encourage early practitioners to venture into that vulnerable space too with curiosity and openness, as Val Vosket (1999) reminds us; "when we are fallible, we are at our most human and when are most human, we are in touch with our greatest potential for helping clients."

Acknowledging a poor outcome felt like a mixture of dread, stuckness and a deep sense of accountability. I define therapy going wrong as situations or moments where I missed something or made an error. Therapy not going as well as expected, is the client who did not engage after one or two sessions or an unexplained ending and moments they or I felt stuck. "It's just not working, things are still the same" or "I feel worse than before," although deflating to hear, the caveat was that the client felt comfortable enough to be able to tell their truth. Responding with conventional answers felt worn and I probably showed the unease, as I was aware how expressive my face can be. In these moments, I also noticed a perplexing feeling, like a rejection. Not wanting to withdraw, I unconsciously focused on working harder for the client and focusing on new interventions and directing it on another path. This caused the client and I to become out of sync and the stuckness appeared which held me back from 'immediacy'. I lost the courage to simply reflect client feelings or disclose my here-and-now feelings, ultimately missing an opportunity to get to the heart of the matter for the client. As Clara Hill (1948) suggests "the inexperienced counsellor may hesitate the use of immediacy or challenge behaviours" which I acknowledged but these openings were met with stuckness. I also noticed myself feeling anxious when clients were either presenting extreme feelings such as numbness or anger and distress in the room. It again felt too overwhelming to hold that space for them. In reaction, I likely dismissed or colluded as I avoided the situation by turning our attention to information and handouts. Or worse; we collide. It felt incongruent; we were out of pace with each other, and I was accountable as power dynamics dictate. My lack of experience and feelings I mistook as imposter syndrome, restricting the client-therapist relationship from progressing.

I ventured down the route of further deliberate practice but there was little improvement in alleviating 'those' feelings and stuckness. I carefully re-considered what qualities I needed to be more effective and evidence pointed towards delving into my way of relating. McLeod (2013) suggests that the "theory of attachment can be used to understand the dynamics of the relationship between client and therapist" and that studies "provided convincing evidence for the role of both client and therapist attachment style in shaping the process of therapy". The lack of experience and insecure base showed up as fragile client-therapist alliance, hesitancy to use specific counselling skills and outside of sessions there were some poor relationships with those I sought support from personally and professionally and a denial of self-care. I revisited my academic learning and what stood out for me was I needed "courage and perseverance so not to avoid difficult issues or emotions" and to explore how I could make use of my "professional self-doubt and self-acceptance."

In a strong client-therapist relationship, ruptures were easier to resolve and handle with candour, changing interventions or even agreeing an ending. Trust and respect developed easily in some client-therapist relationships but others just clashed. I attended a workshop on a pluralistic approach to attachment, which looked at the value of considering the transference and attachment style of both therapist and client relationship. By providing a secure base, we are helping clients consider the way in which they engage with significant relationships in their lives. I had assumed after all the painstaking personal development in training, I was already providing a secure base. In reflection, I noticed how I tended to avoid intimacy, moving into rationalising instead of meeting my emotions and potential to over identify which can be precarious for a wounded healer. My early attachment style was getting in the way of my work and the question I needed to ask was how to minimise the potential of collusion or collision with clients and others. The answers were to be found in "self- awareness and mindfulness, supervision, and personal therapy," (Joyce, P. 2023).

I leant heavily on supervision for guidance. My supervisor was fundamental in supporting me through my processes and creating awareness of areas I needed to develop. Some of these areas I took to other supports such as personal therapy, peer support or learning resources. I learnt the importance for me of having a supervisor who saw me holistically and in a person-centred way. I was able to trust them with my vulnerabilities and be authentic. They essentially helped me develop my own therapist-self rather than become the vision of the therapist I had wanted to be. I explored unconscious processes and attachment with my personal therapist which helped me guiltlessly access self-care, challenge unhelpful core beliefs and improve relationships. I took a pluralistic approach towards searching for a therapist whom I could work with on issues I was dealing with at that time, in a way or cultural resource that worked for me. This time I sought an art therapist who was sensitive and responsive to my culture, to support me through the therapeutic process with a psychodynamic approach. I also embarked on CPD that was enriching both personally and professionally, often turning to audible books which gave me some relief from reading and as part of my self-care I joined groups where I gained support from peers who had values aligned with my own.

Three key takeaways from this experience:

1. **Importance of authentic relationships:** Building an authentic relationship with clients is crucial for effective therapy. It involves being genuine, open, and willing to engage deeply with clients' emotions and experiences. This authenticity helps create a strong client-therapist alliance, which is essential for therapeutic success.

2. **Value of self-awareness and personal development:** Continuous self-reflection and personal development are vital for a therapist's growth. Understanding one's own attachment style, addressing insecurities, and engaging in self-care are necessary steps to become more effective and empathetic in practice. Personal therapy, supervision, and other support systems play a key role in this development. Instilling self-compassion gives the courage to be vulnerable and honest, and the perseverance to explore and learn from challenges. Instilling self compassion gave me courage to be vulnerable and honest and the perseverance to explore and learn from challenges.

3. **Adaptability and pluralistic approach:** Being adaptable and open to different therapeutic approaches can enhance the therapeutic process. Embracing a pluralistic approach that considers the unique needs and preferences of each client, as well as being open to exploring various interventions and methodologies, can lead to better outcomes. The importance of using professional expertise adeptly in the early years of professional practice to support the lack of experience.

How did this experience help you improve your practice?

By working on attachment and emotions, I have freed up and changed personal aspects and traits, allowing my practice and skills to flow more naturally and creating a secure space for clients. This experience has also helped me assert and maintain healthy boundaries in both professional and personal relationships.

Exploring my relationship with my 'self' provided valuable insights into my feelings as a counsellor of colour, particularly through participation in a year-long experiential group focused on somatic healing from racial trauma. This enriching experience allowed me to process the wounded healer part of myself and set boundaries more readily and effortlessly when dealing with issues close to me.

How did supervision support you through the experience? Did you access any additional supports?

Supervision was fundamental in guiding me through this process. My supervisor provided a holistic, person-centred approach that allowed me to explore my vulnerabilities and develop my therapist-self authentically. They helped me identify areas for growth, which I then addressed through personal therapy, peer support, and learning resources. Personal therapy was particularly beneficial, as it helped me access self-care, challenge unhelpful core beliefs, and improve my relationships. I also engaged in CPD activities and joined supportive peer groups, which enriched my personal and professional development.

What insights have you gained from being curious about the experience and from the process of self-reflection?

Curiosity and self-reflection have provided valuable insights into my practice. I learnt the importance of being present and authentic with clients, recognising and addressing my own attachment style, and embracing a pluralistic approach. This process helped me understand the impact of my personal experiences on my professional work and highlighted the need for continuous self-awareness and development. It also emphasised the importance of seeking support from supervision, personal therapy, and peer groups to maintain a healthy balance and avoid burnout.

What guidance and learning would you offer other professionals?

Developing your intuition and therapist reflexivity can be crucial for realising your potential. Insights from Val Wosket's 'The Therapeutic Use of Self,' understanding 'reflexivity' coined by David L. Rennie, and Daryl Chow's research into counselling endings have significantly influenced my development. Reflecting on professional and personal development journals and tutor feedback early can uncover emerging patterns that lead to meaningful learning.

Choosing a supervisor or personal therapist who aligns with your professional and personal needs is vital. An experienced supervisor can provide valuable guidance, especially if you're in the early stages of your career. It's beneficial to discern whether issues brought to supervision are for validation or learning.

When feeling stagnant in practice, self-reflection through writing, peer discussions, or attending CPD can provide new insights and inspirations. Learning to analyse academic research papers helps in choosing sources carefully, creating working materials, and identifying future research areas, keeping your practice adept, fresh, and creative.

In organisations where counselling is not the primary service, familiarity with operational issues like GDPR, safeguarding, and assessment procedures can enhance your work
processes and mitigate therapy risks. Addressing management issues early ensures organised work processes.

Implementing self-care, though it may seem overwhelming, has far-reaching benefits. Regularly checking in with your emotional and physical health and considering personal therapy can prevent compassion fatigue and work stress. Prioritising self-care, even with simple enjoyable activities, and planning it into your schedule ensures it becomes routine. Remember, your needs are as important as anyone else's.

References and Bibliography

Wosket, Val – The Therapeutic Use of Self, 1999. 1 st Ed, published by Routledge.

McLeod, John – An Introduction to Research In Counselling & Psychology, 2013. Sage Publications.

Hill, Clara E. – Helping Skills. 2014, 4 th Edition. American Psychological Association.

Rennie, D. L – Person-Centred Counselling. 1 st Ed, 1998. Sage Publications.

Brown, B. – Daring Greatly. 2018, Penguin Audio.

Professional Practice in Counselling and Psychotherapy, Ethics and Law Peter Jenkins, 2017 First Edition.

"Attachment: A Pluralistic Perspective" workshop by Dr Patricia Joyce, Grounded Learning, 2023

"Selfcare" workshop by Sally Lumsdaine, Abertay University, 2020

"What are the qualities of an effective therapist?" workshop by Julia McLeod, Abertay University, 2019

Chapter Three

Impact not Intentions: The Wounded Healer

Amrita Dash

*"I have come to believe over and over again that what is
most important to me must be spoken, made verbal
and shared, even at the risk of having it
bruised or misunderstood."*
Audre Lorde

About me

I am an integrative therapist, clinical supervisor, and trainer. I practice from an anti-racist, anti-oppressive, intersectional and de-colonial framework. I started my journey as an assistant psychologist a decade ago where I first experienced what being a young woman within a hierarchical power structure in mental health meant and it was one of the pivotal experiences that shaped my identity as a practitioner. Since then, I have completed one-year person centred training, Diploma in CBT and groupwork, Diploma in Supervision additional training in Schema therapy, compassion focused therapy, DBT skills and trauma among others. My approach to therapy is relational and I specialise in working with trauma (including intergenerational and racial trauma) and clients from so called minority populations.

Let me start this chapter by inviting you to pause for a moment and reflect on your response to the phrase, 'when therapy does go wrong?' What thoughts or images cross your mind, what feelings emerge and how does your body react? Take a moment and record these in whichever way that feels right (you may choose to write, draw, doodle, everything is okay. If this isn't accessible you can use another way). You may want to pay particular attention to what words are emerging, the descriptors. Are these descriptors about you as a therapist or practitioner or about the client? Similarly, if you are a client who has had experience of therapy going wrong, are these words more about yourself or the others - including the therapist?

When we hear these words, we can often think of the big transgressions, boundary violations and safeguarding failures. While these are all relevant and true, we can often fail to account for the missed opportunities of contact, relational attunement or inability to hold our own process (as therapists) that causes significant and accumulative harm. This is what this chapter is going to explore in terms of therapy going wrong – harm. What is it and how do we work with the idea that we can cause it even with the best of intentions. While discussing harm within therapy, clinicians can lean towards thinking about failure in meeting treatment outcomes, scores not changing, re-traumatisation, decrease in functionality. Again, all very important points to consider but, what about the relational needs and the 'little harms' of everyday sessions? When do they add up to a big harm? Why do we as people sometimes get stuck at 'well that wasn't their intention'? We hear this narrative commonly through all our social discourse especially if one finds oneself at one or more intersections. What happens when the impact limits our ways of having a dialogue about intentions?

I wonder if we as therapists shy away from discussing harm and focus on intentions because the dictionary definition of it has an element of deliberateness to it. I believe it is fair to accept that most therapists train to become so with genuine care and even love for the people they want to work with. Is that enough? It is not always useful to only think in terms of intentions as professionals, as most people train and practice with great intentions and empathy. For instance, when we discuss guilt with clients we often would talk about intent and rightly so to be able to support clients to let go of things they are not responsible for. Things which are often handed down from others. However, as a professional operating with an anti-oppressive framework, I firmly believe that good intentions are not enough. We need active reflections of our power, positionality, world views and process. Sounds obvious, doesn't it?

Let's take another moment of stillness and with curiosity inquire 'who decides when or how therapy has gone wrong'. Is it the therapist? The client? Or do we come to this conclusion collaboratively, separately? What happens after this point?

I put this question to my colleagues, catching some of them by surprise. For some it depends on the modality -it is the responsibility of the therapist to ensure they are constantly examining the process. For others it is the client or a joint effort. All the above can be true and yet none of them may actually be used in practice. Because if it was truly practised that all therapists were responsibly engaging in the process and clients were responded to in terms of harm caused, the phrases like 'avoidant', 'resistant', 'not ready' and 'non-compliant' would not be readily used. Now add in the layer of intersectionality where cultural factors, racial inequality, poverty, non-normative gender presentations, sexuality or neurodivergence is not accounted for.

Now a last question; what is your relationship with power? Please take some time to write, draw or record in another way how you relate to power in general or power as a therapist.

> *"There are many kinds of power, used and unused, ac-*
> *knowledged or otherwise."*
> *Audre Lorde*

I do not subscribe to the rigid idea of the inherent power differential that only therapists hold the power and clients do not. In my mind, that is too simplistic an idea and makes power this static, solid thing which it is not. I do, however, propose that therapists do hold power and often can have power just by being able to meet some of the clients' needs. I often invite my students to consider spaces in their lives where they have such undivided attention, acceptance and visibility and the impact of it especially if it's rare. There is immense power in that for both the client and the therapist. Therefore, we must consider how power and needs intersect. There are times and opportunities when we know our power, our identities, but because of having some of our needs met, we may choose to, or be forced, to let all or some of our power go. When does this become oppression and then alienation? Minikin (2018) explores the idea that oppression, mystification and isolation lead to alienation. Again, with ideas of oppression we think of big active events, not the daily occurrences even from within us from our internalised oppressors.

While thinking about my contribution for this book I considered many ideas; stories where I have failed to meet clients' needs; where I have misjudged a presentation and when I have been out of my depth. However, the idea that kept making itself at home within my mind and body was where I was a client. I struggled initially both with the thought of being vulnerable but also to make it relevant. The fact remained that by finding myself drawn again and again to this experience, I thought I must acknowledge the parallel process and give it shape. As I write this, I can almost hear the critics going… "well of course it impacted you, it was personal." I ask that you stay with me. It also felt relevant as in this engagement, I was never fully the client. In fact, my therapist had noted multiple times how it felt to them that a session was like they were talking to a colleague (which in general terms professionally we were) and 'to let them be the therapist' (often as a joke). Our professional frame became too blurred. It feels important to see it through the lens of the client to illustrate how much the implicit power in the therapeutic relationship can disempower even the most assertive of clients if not met with care and awareness. After all, "the most potent weapon in the hands of the oppressor is the mind of the oppressed" (Biko, 1978, p.68)

And lastly, because no other recent experience has had such a profound impact on my practice than this one. The old, wounded healer paradigm (Jung 1944). It is the unmet needs that often shape the script of our lives.

Before we fully embark upon the story, it also feels important to say that this exploration is offered with humility and vulnerability. I will describe my therapist in vague terms to honour their confidentiality. This isn't about finding a villain for this story or me not stepping up to take accountability. It simply is my truth and the learning I took away from this experience. I am going to use the framework of Erskine's relational needs and ethical principles of psychotherapy (Cottone and Tarvydas 2016) for this.

As a woman of colour feminist practitioner, I made conscious and deliberate choices about finding a therapist who would be able to meet me on specific intersections of race, experience and practice. This was challenging in itself, finding someone who would meet my relational need of mutuality and confirmation of personal experience (Erskine and Traut mann 1996). I wanted to engage in therapy to explore the impact of childhood trauma, family dynamics and deepen my understanding of my own process. To put it in perspective, in total I worked almost two years online with the therapist privately on either a fortnightly or weekly basis. Through this journey I discovered many wonderful and some hurtful things about myself. I am grateful for all of them.

At first, working with the therapist everything felt fine. I felt seen, heard, and acknowledged. I had disclosed some of the trauma I wanted to explore early on, so we had shared knowledge of key incidents and dynamics. Throughout the therapy, they would comment on what a sophisticated thinker I was and what a unique way of being I had as well as being so articulate that people listened to me. They were, in the language of transactional analysis, 'the wonderful warm fuzzies'! As you can imagine, this deeply met my need of being validated and affirmed as significant (Erskine and Trautmann 1996). This has been something I had deeply sought in the past. Firstly as a brown girl growing up in an overtly patriarchal society and later as an immigrant trying to carve my personal and professional space in a new country where I was seen as 'other'. During our sessions we would often speak about my approach to my practice, and this is where I wonder if some of the blurring of the boundaries began as we ended up talking theories and ideas as peers. I still struggle not to take responsibility for it, not to believe that because I am an experienced practitioner I 'should' have known better. This is of course part of my process that I went to therapy for in the first place. If that was shared by a client to me, or my supervisees brought this to me, I would firmly state that in this equation the primary responsibility of maintaining ethical responsibility and holding the professional frame remains with the therapist.

Over time, the boundaries became more porous. I had asked several times for them to confirm with me the number of sessions we had completed. I never got an answer, they would joke and tell me that they kept forgetting and this doesn't happen for them with anyone else, just me. I was assured they would let me know but weren't able to follow through on their promise (principle of promise keeping and veracity; Cottone and Tarvydas 2016).

They would on occasion tell me they had taken me to supervision because I manage to confound them so easily. I think this fed into my need to make an impact on an other and made me special (Erskine and Trautmann, 1996). While there may be arguments, we can explore the use of supervision with clients, again here both of us laughed at it and the theme of humour continued. Looking at it now, I wonder about the principles of beneficence and fairness (Cottone and Tarvydas 2016).

So, while perhaps the need to be seen continued, the need for security kept increasing as it felt less and less reliable (Erskine and Trautmann 1996). As the sessions were online, after the first year they would forget to send me links before the session, and I had to text at the time of many sessions asking if they are still on and that I don't have a link. Once, they asked me to set up the link and send it to them. Altogether, trampling on my need for the other to initiate (Erskine and Trautmann 1996). Not big transgressions individually but drip, drip, drip and the bucket overflows.

During the last few months of therapy, their diary had significantly changed. They asked for a change of time which I agreed to, but the connection wasn't stable so session after session we struggled to connect.

When I had addressed this, it was the internet, or the change in diary but not them. At this point not only was the security almost non-existent, but the dependable other - who had been affirming me - was acting as though I was making a big deal out of nothing. I offered that since this was being so challenging we could take a break and return when their dairy had gone back to previous availability. They responded that this had already happened and there shouldn't be any issues going ahead. Reading this you may ask, why didn't I just go to a different therapist? I could have, but the idea of starting over again with someone else at this point felt exhausting. I already felt exhausted from this balancing act and the reality of having some of my needs met and mutuality of experience kept me there. I have tried to transcribe, to the best of my ability, a last key conversation I had with them which stayed with me for a while. As something that had been offered originally as warm and fuzzy; turned into 'the cold shoulder.'

Me: I have been struggling with all the time changes and cancellations.

Therapist: yes, the connection recently has been quite bad.

Me: well, I can understand that with your current circumstances. Why don't you let me know when your diary is more able for us to resume.

Therapist: yeah, it's all good now.

Second half of the session:

Me: Talking about a challenge with a colleague.

Therapist: this is what I mean that you are a sophisticated thinker and people listen to you. Earlier when you were talking about changes etc, I should have just said to you 'take it or leave it.'

Here, I believe they unconsciously re-enacted something from my past (which they were aware of as we had spoken about it many times). This can happen in any therapeutic relationship – it's known as the rupture. At this juncture I didn't know what else I could do to repair the relationship (yes, I hear myself!). This was the theme I had been holding on to - it's okay, it's a rupture we can work through this. This happens, my therapist is human (this is an example of me never fully being the client). After the session, we agreed to a date which they changed. I agreed to a new date and didn't hear from them that week or the next week or the next. This time I decided to express love (Erskine and Trautmann 1996) for myself and not send a message reminding them of our commitment. They finally reached out to me five weeks later saying the thing about the diary change has happened now, contradicting the previous communication (Veracity, Cottone and Travydas 2016).

Not once did I then, or now, believe my therapist had anything but the best of intentions for me or their practice. The impact however, was a different story. While this narrative isn't something I needed to necessarily take to supervision, perhaps continuing on the theme of me taking too much responsibility – I ended up taking this to both my supervisors to whom I owe gratitude for their support to heal holistically. They held me as a person while also allowing me to explore what this means professionally for me.

I decided to take a step back and explore what I had learnt, how I had let my power go and the impact it had. It led me to look at my own practice in all my roles, and ways I addressed, as well as understood, harm with a critical eye. I learnt the art of letting go and the idea that all the knowledge I held as a practitioner 'should' have helped me make better decisions as a client. If someone had asked me the questions I asked at the beginning of the chapter, I would have said "huh, I can write books on power my friend," (and I can), I understand all the intersections and identify oppression. This all being true has shown me how much I still have to learn. While discussing this chapter, one of my supervisors asked me how I would feel if my clients read it. My response at first was 'vulnerable' which is true but also, if it would help a client to speak with me about harm I may have caused, then I have achieved my objective. I wish I could offer one cohesive definition of harm but alas, like power, it's not one thing. It needs our continuous attention, openness to explore our process, engage with our own defences and fragility, and our ability to listen to the spoken as well as unspoken ways clients are telling us about their experience.

In the end I have assimilated this experience into my narrative with the help of one of my favourite Urdu couplets:

'Kyon darein zindagi mein kya hoga,' 'why fear what will happen in life Kuch na hoga toh tazurba hoga'. 'If nothing else experience will.'
- Javed Akhtar

Three key takeaways from this experience:

1. **Impact over intentions:** It's crucial to prioritise the impact of our actions over our intentions. Despite good intentions, therapists can cause harm through overlooked or unaddressed issues in the therapeutic relationship. Understanding and mitigating this harm requires continuous self-reflection and an openness to receive feedback from clients.

2. **Power dynamics and boundaries:** Therapists must remain vigilant about maintaining professional boundaries and recognising the power dynamics inherent in the therapist-client relationship. Even experienced practitioners can struggle with these boundaries, highlighting the importance of ongoing self-awareness and boundary management.

3. **Importance of reliable, consistent practice:** Consistency and reliability in therapy sessions are fundamental to building trust and security for clients. Frequent changes, cancellations, or lapses in communication can significantly undermine the therapeutic relationship and the client's sense of safety.

How did this experience help you improve your practice?

This experience underscored the importance of balancing empathy with professional boundaries and highlighted the necessity of being attuned to the client's needs beyond the obvious treatment goals. It also reinforced the value of reflecting on the therapeutic process from both the therapist's and client's perspectives, promoting a more holistic and client-centred approach to practice.

How did clinical supervision support you through the experience? Did you access any additional supports?

Supervision provided a vital space for processing the complexities of the situation, allowing for emotional support and professional guidance. The supervisors offered a balanced perspective, validating the emotional impact while also encouraging critical reflection on professional practices. This support was crucial for integrating the experience into a framework of learning and growth.

What insights have you gained from being curious about the experience and from the process of self-reflection?

- **Continuous learning and growth:** Being curious and open to self-reflection revealed the ongoing nature of learning in therapeutic practice. It highlighted the need for humility and the recognition that even experienced therapists must remain open to new insights and self improvement.
- **Power is fluid, not static:** Understanding that power dynamics in therapy are complex and fluid, rather than fixed, helped in appreciating the nuances of each therapeutic interaction. This insight fosters a more subtle approach to handling power within the therapeutic relationship.
- **Self-compassion and professional responsibility:** Balancing self-compassion with professional responsibility is essential. Accepting one's own vulnerabilities and mistakes as a therapist while striving for continuous improvement enhances the therapeutic process for both the client and the therapist.

What guidance and learning would you offer other professionals?

- **Prioritise impact over intentions:** Always consider the actual impact of your actions on clients. Good intentions are not enough if the impact is harmful. Actively seek and respond to client feedback to ensure their needs are being met.

- **Maintain professional boundaries:** Vigilantly uphold professional boundaries to protect the integrity of the therapeutic relationship. Be aware of the subtle ways boundaries can blur and take proactive steps to maintain them.
- **Commit to consistency and reliability:** Ensure therapy sessions are consistent and reliable. Clients need to feel secure and trust that their therapist will be present and dependable.
- **Engage in regular supervision:** Utilise supervision not just for case management but for personal and professional reflection. Supervision can offer critical insights and support for navigating complex therapeutic dynamics.
- **Embrace vulnerability and openness:** Be open to discussing your own vulnerabilities and mistakes. This openness can enhance your practice and model healthy processing of challenges for your clients.
- **Reflect on power dynamics:** Continuously reflect on power dynamics in your therapeutic relationships. Recognise the fluidity of power and strive to create a balanced, collaborative therapeutic environment.

By integrating these insights and practices, therapists can better navigate the complexities of their roles, ultimately fostering more effective and compassionate therapeutic relationships.

References:

Biko, S. (1978). I write what I like. Selected writings by Steve Biko. Chicago, IL: University of Chicago Press.

Cottone, R.R , Tarvydas, V. (2016). Ethics and decision making on counselling and psychotherapy (4 th ed.). Springer publishing co.

Erskine, R. G. & Trautmann, R. L. (1996). Methods of an Integrative Psychotherapy. In R. G.

Erskine, *Theories and methods of an integrative transactional analysis: A volume of selected articles.* (pp.20-36). San Francisco: TA Press. (Original work published 1996, Transactional Analysis Journal, 26: 316-328.)

Jung, C.G. (1944). Psychology of the unconscious. London

Minkin, K. (2018). Radical Relational Psychiatry: Toward a democracy of mind and people.

Transactional Analysis Journal, 48: 2, 111-125

A special thanks to Bev Gibbons and Satinder Panesar for encouraging me to write my truth. To my colleagues for answering me honestly and candidily when I asked random questions. Lastly, to Erin Stevens who has inspired some of my thinking around harm in therapy through her social media.

Chapter Four

Misinterpretation of Unconscious Process: Turning Misunderstanding into Opportunity for Growth

Michelle McQuillan

By way of an introduction, I shall start by telling you a little about myself, my journey into the wonderful world of therapy, and the way in which I practice. I have always been interested in how the mind works and in therapy in general, but my interests shifted more to therapy in practice after finding myself in a major life transitioning period. In 2006 I was diagnosed with, treated for, and survived cancer. In the attempt to spare my family and friends from the turmoil of the emotional rollercoaster ride that goes hand-in-hand with this type of existential crisis, my search turned to professional support. I quickly became acutely aware of how little help there appeared to be available for people in my situation, which led me to wonder whether I could contribute in some small way to bridge that gap. Fast forward a number of years, an ongoing journey of learning, self-discovery and self-awareness, and I found myself taking the opportunity to complete a Person-Centred and Experiential MSc. in Counselling and Psychotherapy. I was drawn to this modality because I believe wholeheartedly in the purity of the belief that we all hold the answers we seek, if only we can reach them; that being seen, heard and witnessed, without judgement, for who we are at our core can transform us; and that learning to love ourselves for who we are, rather than who we are expected to be, can help us to live a more peaceful and authentic life.

In the very early, recently qualified days of my practice as a therapist, I worked with a young male client, who shall be called Tony (not his real name), and who gave me his explicit consent to use anonymised material from his therapy. Tony said the words "so you're fed up with me now too" mid conversation. My initial 'newly qualified, not good enough' reaction was that I had drifted off and missed some really important information. In the moment I felt I could do one of two things... go along with it and hope that Tony didn't notice, or I could be genuine and congruent in an attempt to maintain and build on the therapeutic relationship we had been building. Thankfully, I chose the latter. My rationale was that if I was less than honest, the relationship would be very damaged, and the trust would be gone. However, if I was honest, even if I was at fault, any potential rupture in the relationship could be more easily repaired due to me taking accountability and responsibility and demonstrating the art of reparative communication. As Tony had stopped talking, I said, "I'm sorry who said that?" and the response he gave was, "You. You sighed, so you are obviously fed up with me too." The reality from my perspective was that I was struggling with my breathing due to asthma, and I had unconsciously taken a deep breath. However, from Tony's perspective, when he experiences 'a sigh' it is assigned the meaning of 'I'm fed up with you.' My impulse was to correct Tony's perspective in favour of my own, as much to let myself 'off the hook,' as for Tony's emotional regulation. However, in seeing the effect in Tony, his body language, his silence, his demeanour, the pulse in his cheek visually throbbing, it became very clear that this was a real distress for him. He appeared to be really struggling to contain it. This situation/reaction took place about eight minutes from the end of the session and so we sat in silence. I was not well versed in silence at this stage in my development, so it was very uncomfortable for me, and I was also concerned that it might be too much for Tony. Yet my reflexive instinct or gut reaction, was that this was VERY important. As we came to the end of the session, me willing Tony to feel accepted in his distress without voicing it, and Tony still struggling with tolerating his distress, I reminded him we had a few minutes left and asked him if he wished to book another appointment. He replied with an (almost) defiant "Yes."

I was devastated. I questioned everything I had done and said. I was sure I would never see Tony again. Or worse, that I had damaged him in some way. That night I called and spoke with my clinical supervisor, horrified that I had 'scared' Tony off and he would NEVER return! Of course, to my mind this was all my fault! If Tony had a 'more experienced' therapist, that situation would never have happened. My amazing clinical upervisor calmed me down and was able to see past my internal dialogue. He encouraged me to see what seeds had been sown for Tony, that he could be accepted, even in a distressed state, perhaps for the first time. And of course, there was clearly a parallel process for me feeling not good enough as a therapist yet, right alongside Tony feeling not good enough as a client. There is an important point to be made here. We are both looking at this same situation, but we are seeing very different things. Tony's unconscious process is filtering the incoming information (the sigh) through his core belief system, and I am filtering the information through mine (completely unaware I had taken a deep breath let alone that it had been so misinterpreted). I had to now consider that even the most microscopic unconscious process like a breath, deep or otherwise, can be seen very differently than intended. The message we are trying to convey may and can be very different from the messages received based on these nuanced unconscious processes.

However, something had shifted! Tony returned, much to my surprise, so that went some way to helping me reconsider my perspective. Maybe I could trust my instincts. And maybe, just maybe, I had handled the situation well enough for him to feel able, and in fact welcome, to return to therapy. Moreover, perhaps something had shifted in Tony too. Afterall, despite barely tolerating his distress during his previous appointment, here he was, back in the room! It might be prudent here to consider the power imbalance in this situation… As Tony came in for therapy initially there appeared to be a deference to my 'knowledge and qualifications' based on surreptitious questions Tony asked such as "What do you think?," "Is this normal?" and more overt statements such as "You tell me, you're the expert." In these moments, offering Tony those same questions and statements back, with gentle curiosity, appeared to somewhat alleviate any power imbalance Tony might have perceived. So, my perception of Tony returning to therapy was that he felt safe enough (if a little defiant) in the therapeutic relationship despite the rupture and was testing the boundaries within that. However, he also attempted to assert his own power in the answers he gave when any questions were put back to him, which he reported felt new to him. And, of course, there were times when it was very tempting for me to say "Well, I think…" but what would Tony actually gain from that… another person with expectations of him, more rules to comply with, more conditions to his worth? (Rogers, 1959) These are very important aspects to consider in every interaction or intervention in therapy. Everything we do and say can be misinterpreted. I don't say this to scaremonger, more to raise awareness that putting these questions back to Tony helped him to formulate his own, more authentic opinions which were right for him rather than concoct new ways of being in order to please others. In this case, me.

After we had both landed in the room upon Tony's return, and at the risk of being perceived as directive, I said to Tony "Our last appointment appeared to end on a very difficult note for you, and also for me, so I wonder if it is something you want to explore?" My rationale for this was two-fold: 1) acknowledging the rupture in order to create a safe and congruent space from where Tony could choose, or not, to participate in rupture repair and 2) creating an opportunity for Tony to get curious about where his core belief came from and perhaps find ways to manage or alleviate the distress he feels as a result of it. And for me, this appeared to be an opportunity to facilitate Tony in taking back his power, both in session with me and beyond, in order to learn how to navigate his emotions and find coping strategies that resonated with him rather than those around him. Tony was very keen to discuss what happened, and he reported thinking things through and realising that often, when his mother used the words "I'm fed up with you now" it was invariable delivered with a sigh, which Tony took to indicate the conversation or interaction was over from his mother's perspective, which he reported left him feeling worthless. So, when he experienced my deep breath, which was imperceptible to me, it was very audible to him and raised within him the 'assumption' that I too was fed up with him. Further, it led to a consideration that perhaps Tony might be making 'assumptions' in other areas of his life too. The whole time Tony was going through his process, I was very aware of my inclination to explain myself, and to rescue him, but again my reflexive instinct was to stay within Tony's frame of reference and let it play out for him in his own time.

In the process of my own development as a therapist I came across the psychological concept of 'epoché.' The philosopher, Edmund Husserl, (Walsh, 1988) adopted this psychological term which he suggested means "…to suspend judgement" and he redefined it somewhat to espouse "bracketing… of naïve consciousness in favour of the phenomenologically 'reduced' point of view." Similarly, for the purposes of this chapter, I redefine this same term to define my own process of "bracketing" in terms of my own personal reactions and feelings, which are about me and my life, in these sessions with Tony as a way of putting it to one side, to deal with in my private Clinical Supervision later. This ensures I intentionally stay within Tony's frame of reference during his sessions. However, it is important to make the distinction here between my own process, versus what is coming up for me about Tony's contribution to the sessions. For example, I might use immediacy about 'my confusion' around conflicting information I hear from Tony or when I notice he is saying one thing but emoting another. This can be a very useful and effective way of fostering an open and honest communication with Tony, despite being in a space where he has experienced distress and discomfort before. Due to the trust built through repairing the rupture, Tony appeared to feel safe enough to listen and to respond equally openly and honestly, which offered him the opportunity for personal growth. Equally, this was an opportunity for me to reflect on whether what was coming up for me was indeed mine… meaning it has touched something in my own personal experience, which would be an example of when I practice epoché; or whether I am picking up something from Tony... perhaps some cognitive dissonance. For example, while Tony was exploring things which appeared to me to be extremely traumatic, he would sometimes smile or even laugh while relating his difficulties. This effectively minimised his experience and I realised that this might be contributing to the difficulties he reported experiencing in his relationships, both in therapy and in life. But the big player here, for me, is knowing oneself as a therapist. To identify this as my reaction to the incongruent information being received, in the moment, versus the client's accounts of their experience hitting my own experiences. Self-awareness is key to understanding this process in action. The ability to be reflective in real time as well as with hindsight; to be open (and brave) enough to raise any concerns in the moment using immediacy and curiosity. Meanwhile monitoring any other visual or auditory cues which may be unconsciously omitted (back to the sigh!), for example, my hard or soft tone and/or my hard or soft face, but also, and perhaps most importantly, remembering that as well as being a therapist in the room, I am first and foremost a human being, who can't possibly get it right every time. Which moves me on nicely to my next major concept... the art of self-compassion and self-forgiveness if, and when, I do get things wrong.

Self-compassion can at times feel elusive. Our seemingly negatively biased brains have evolved to take in that which confirms our existing core beliefs about ourselves and the world and ignore that which negates them, otherwise known as the 'Confirmation Bias' (Wason, 1960). As such it is very easy to find oneself down a rabbit-hole of self-derision and unconstructive criticism. This might make self-compassion seem out of reach and yet, as with everything, knowledge is key to learning this new skill, practice is key to developing it, and consistently applying the practice is key to honing it.

So, what is self-compassion, and more importantly how do we access it? According to Dr Kristen Neff (2020) there are "three elements to compassion". Firstly, we must "notice" the suffering of others; secondly, we need to "feel moved" by the suffering; and finally, we need to recognise that "suffering is part of the human experience." Once we fully appreciate that, we can then view ourselves in the same way as we view others. Dr Neff suggests when we recognise "this is really difficult right now… and how can I comfort and care for myself in this moment?" … "instead of mercilessly judging and criticising yourself for… inadequacies or shortcomings" it affords us the opportunity to "turn compassion inwards" and give self-compassion to yourself when faced with personal failings. Sounds easy, right? Wrong! I have found this to be one of the most difficult and elusive concepts to grasp and apply, both in the therapy room, and outside of it. However, in my view, it is imperative that we as therapists continue to strive for this particular skill. As seen earlier, with 'the sigh,' our clients pick up on the smallest of nuances in the room. The therapeutic relationship is as much an example of a 'healthy way to relate' as it is an environment which is conducive to personal growth. How can we possibly claim to have a desire for our clients to grow and flourish using their newly learnt skills if we, as therapists, don't practice what we preach and demonstrate how to do it? If I had intervened with Tony any earlier during our uncomfortable session, neither of us would have had the growth experience we gained, and Tony could easily have thought "oh yeah, do as I say, not as I do" and never returned. Instead, trusting my reflexive instinct afforded us both an opportunity to learn and grow.

Fast forward five years and I am in a room with a different client, who says out loud "… you are picking at your fingers, like you are angry at what I'm saying." Déjà vu! I am catapulted back in time, into that room with Tony, only this time, I am starting from a place of experience. This time I am able to ask, "You think I'm angry because I am picking at my fingers?" This time, I know it's because I bent my nail back before the session started and I'm unconsciously touching it whilst resisting the urge to bite it. Yet this time I feel less inclined to defend myself and rescue my client. And, this time, I know what to do… I stay with my client, in his frame of reference. This time, I trust my reflexive instinct and we more easily go on a journey of self-discovery for the client where we can test out what is going on for him. Where that core belief that if I'm picking at my fingers it means I'm 'angry with him' came from and together we are able to check out where else in this client's life he makes these assumptions based on his core beliefs. While unconstructive criticism is still an issue for me, it carries a lot less clout, and I have learnt, over time and experience, that it can be more usefully used as a tool for self-development than for one of self-derision.

According to the Oxford dictionary, the definition of 'therapy' is "the treatment of mental conditions by verbal communication and interaction" (Simpson & Weiner, 2000). For me, therapy is indicative of the Gestalt concept that something is more than the sum of its parts. For me, therapy is a safe space, it is a therapeutic relationship, it is a mutual endeavour to reach relational depth (Cooper, 2020), sometimes for the first time; where we can test out how things might be if patterns are adapted, reconfigured, or amended at a pace that suits the client. It is an exciting opportunity to discover who we really are in the depth of our being which we know as 'self.'

Which neatly circles back to my choice of modality. The wholehearted belief in the purity that we can find the answers we seek, if we look within; that being seen, heard and witnessed, without judgement, for who we are at our core, affords the opportunity, to transform us, both in the room and out of it; and, finally that learning to love ourselves for who we are, rather than who we are expected to be, can help us to live a more peaceful and authentic life.

In conclusion, it feels prudent that we consider that it is imperative we bring our whole self into the room when working with clients. Our training teaches us the skills to create a safe space, to meet the client where they are, to use our experiences as a foundation to understand those of our client, while retaining focus on the client. But what it cannot teach us, is how and when to trust our instincts. That is the work we as individual therapists must learn to do ourselves. The good news is that it does get easier with time and experience. However, that does not mean we can become complacent. Every client experience is different. Every interaction holds as much of a learning opportunity for us as therapists as it does for our clients. For me, this ongoing journey of learning, self-discovery and self-awareness is exactly that; ongoing. So, I'll end with the thought that in writing this chapter, it has helped me reflect on and consolidate what I have learnt about myself as a person and as a therapist over the years. I have grown in both domains, thanks to those I have worked with, clients and colleagues alike, and that growth has helped me gain confidence in what I do. I will not always get it right, but I will always endeavour to work on, and learn from ruptures and repairs and I will always bring my whole self into the therapeutic space, otherwise I would be doing my clients a grave disservice. Equally, I will continue to work on self-compassion. It is necessary in this amazing, sometimes traumatic, but always privileged position that we as therapists hold in society. It is an honour, and deeply humbling, that clients afford us the opportunity to see parts of their lives which they do not share with others. My hope for the reader is that in reading this chapter, it will bring hope to those who struggle with self-belief as a therapist, and self-compassion when things go wrong. If you only take one thing away from your time reading this chapter, I hope it is that you can absolutely trust your reflexive instincts!

Three key takeaways from this experience:

1. **Trust in reflexive instincts:** The experience highlighted the importance of trusting one's reflexive instincts as a therapist. Genuine reactions even when uncomfortable, can foster deeper therapeutic relationships and create opportunities for growth and understanding for both the client and the therapist.
2. **Power of rupture and repair:** The incident with Tony demonstrated that ruptures in the therapeutic relationship, when handled with honesty and openness, can be pivotal moments for building trust and facilitating significant personal growth.

3. **Role of Self-Compassion:** Developing self-compassion is crucial for therapists. Accepting and learning from mistakes without harsh self-criticism enhances the therapist's ability to remain present and effective in their practice.

How did this experience help you improve your practice?

This experience improved my practice by reinforcing the necessity of staying present with the client and valuing their frame of reference. It taught me the significance of non-defensive communication and the benefits of allowing clients to process their experiences without premature intervention. Additionally, it deepened my understanding of the subtle dynamics in the therapeutic relationship, such as how unconscious signals can be misinterpreted based on a client's past experiences.

How did clinical supervision support you through the experience? Did you access any additional supports?

Supervision provided crucial support by offering a different perspective on the incident with Tony. My supervisor helped me reframe the situation from one of self-blame to one of mutual learning and growth. This guidance was invaluable in helping me see the positive aspects of the rupture and repair process. Additionally, the supervision sessions emphasised the importance of self-compassion and reflective practice. While I did not access additional supports formally, the supervisory relationship itself was a critical resource.

What insights have you gained from being curious about the experience and from the process of self-reflection?

Curiosity and self-reflection have provided deep insights into the dynamics of therapeutic interactions. I learnt that even minor, unconscious actions can significantly impact clients, shaped by their past experiences and core beliefs. Reflecting on these moments allows for greater empathy and understanding. This process also underscored the importance of differentiating between the therapist's reactions and the client's projections, helping to maintain a clear focus on the client's needs and experiences.

What guidance and learning would you offer other professionals?

To other professionals, I would offer the following guidance:

- **Embrace mistakes as learning opportunities:** View ruptures in the therapeutic relationship as chances for growth and deepening trust. Approach these moments with honesty and openness.

- **Cultivate self-compassion:** Be kind to yourself and recognise that making mistakes is part of the learning process. Developing self-compassion enables you to be more present and effective with clients.

- **Stay curious and reflective:** Regularly engage in self-reflection and be curious about your own reactions and the client's perspectives. This practice enhances self-awareness and improves therapeutic outcomes.

- **Utilise supervision:** Actively use supervision to gain new perspectives and support. Supervisors can provide valuable insights and help reframe challenging situations constructively.

- **Be authentic:** Bring your whole self into the therapeutic space. Authenticity fosters trust and creates a safe environment for clients to explore their experiences.

These key takeaways and insights emphasise the continuous journey of learning and growth in the practice of therapy, highlighting the importance of self-awareness, empathy, and the therapeutic relationship.

References:

Relational depth: Some frequently asked questions — Mick Cooper training and consultancy. (2020, October 3). Mick Cooper Training and Consultancy. https://mick-cooper.squarespace.com/new-blog/2017/10/10/relational-depth-some-frequently-asked-questions

Neff, K. (2020, July 9). *Definition and three elements of self-compassion,* Kristin Neff. Self-Compassion. https://self-compassion.org/the-three-elements-of-self-compassion-2/

Rogers C (1959) 'A Theory of Therapy, Personality, and Interpersonal Relationships, As Developed in the Client-Centered Framework', in Koch S (ed) (1959)

Simpson, J., Deputy Chief Editor Oxford English Dictionary Edmund Weiner, & Weiner, E. (2000). Oxford English dictionary. In *undefined*. Oxford University Press, USA.

Walsh, R. D. (1988). Husserl's & Epoche as method and truth. *Auslegung: a Journal of Philosophy,* 14(2), 211. https://doi.org/10.17161/ajp.1808.9170

Wason, P. C. (1960). On the failure to eliminate hypotheses in a conceptual task. Quarterly Journal of Experimental Psychology, 12, 129-140.

Chapter Five

Navigating Challenges in Therapy:
Lessons from Unexpected Outcomes

Stephen Queen

I am Stephen Queen, and I have been practising as a Cognitive Behavioural Therapist (CBT) for eight years. I am qualified to master level, accredited with the BABCP **(British Association for Behavioural and Cognitive Psychotherapies.** BACP and NCPS, and I have also gained accreditation as a clinical supervisor with the BABCP. Over the last eight years, I have incorporated other therapeutic modalities into my practice and have qualified in EMDR (Eye Movement Desensitization and Reprocessing), Schema, Hypnosis and Neuro-feedback. I have completed training in working with children and young people and have a speciality in working with sex and porn addiction and POCD **(Paedophilic Obsessive-Compulsive Disorder - it refers to a subtype of Obsessive-Compulsive Disorder (OCD) where individuals experience intrusive, unwanted, and distressing thoughts or fears about the possibility of being a paedophile/paedophilic, despite having no desire to act on such thoughts and often finding them deeply upsetting. These obsessions can lead to significant anxiety and compulsive behaviours. POCD is not an indication of actual paedophilia but rather a mental health condition requiring appropriate treatment).** Before becoming a CBT therapist, I spent 25 years in the construction supply industry and gathered a wealth of experience in business management. This experience helps me add coaching elements to my therapeutic work and has enabled me to work at the boardroom level with charities and businesses.

Having engaged in therapy myself in my late 20s, my eyes were opened to the value of talking therapies. Had it not been for my positive experiences in my therapeutic journey, I would likely never have commenced my training and subsequent career change.

However, that said, my first-ever therapy session was a truly awful experience, where the therapist was more interested in hearing the deep dark details of my childhood abuse, leaving me feeling exposed, hurt, and angry, and I vowed never to have therapy again. That was the first and last session with that therapist, but a friend convinced me to try again, and with their help, I found a fantastic therapist who taught me the true value of the therapeutic relationship.

A difficult case

I recall an experience with a young client who was 14 at the time. The client had been referred via their parent's health insurance for anxiety and symptoms of depression. The initial assessment had gone well, and it was clear that the client would benefit from therapy, but there didn't appear to be any 'keystone' events which would have accounted for the client's high levels of anxiety. After four sessions of building rapport and understanding the client's formulation, I felt confident an underlying condition was causing the client's anxiety, which was, in turn, causing the client's depressive symptoms. The client struggled to articulate goals and noted that they "just wanted to feel better." There was an absence of emotional literacy, and this was within the client's awareness. The client talked about their lifelong difficulties in expressing their emotions and understanding the feelings of others.

I continued to formulate with the client and, at session six, had a review session with the client and their parents. I enquired about the client's early years and gathered that the client experienced delayed language and movement. I was already aware that the client considered themselves to have unusual eating habits and shared sensory issues related to textures, taste, touch, and sound. The client's sensory sound problems were so significant that he used special earplugs at school to help reduce the noise levels. Given the client's avoidant eye contact, stimming, and heightened sensitivity, I was confident that the client's anxiety was driven by autism. With the client's permission, I shared their case formulation with their parents and broached that the client would likely benefit from an autism assessment.

I could see that the client appeared intrigued, as if they had already known that they could be autistic, but the intrigue quickly changed to a look of sadness when the client's mother announced her shock. The client's mother was a schoolteacher and was quick to challenge the case formulation, pointing out that if her child had autism, she'd know as she "works with autistic children all the time". I explained that I was not diagnosing the client but was ethically minded in sharing my therapeutic concern, suggesting that an assessment would be beneficial.

During the review, the client's father remained calm and listened intently while trying to soothe his now very irate wife. The conversation was not going in a positive direction, and the client appeared increasingly uncomfortable with every second. I asked if the client would like to sit in the waiting room, and they quickly left. After that, I listened as the client's mother expressed her disappointment in the service and noted that she hadn't brought her child to be labelled and only wanted them to feel less anxious.

Try as I might, there was no initial resolution, and I suggested I email the parents with some information on autism. I also suggested that the parents look at the client's old school reports and consider if there were any themes or comments that might support the possibility of autism. There was no formal agreement from the client's mother, but their father agreed. I inquired if continuing the work with the client was still okay. The mother said she'd consider it.

I informed the parents that I would email them a summary of our session and an outline of the symptoms and formulation of autism. The client was silent when leaving the building and looked visibly sad. I worked late that evening and sent the email as agreed. Some days later, I received a brief email stating that the client would attend their session as usual, but no further information was added.

The client arrived for the next session with their father. The client immediately took themselves upstairs into the office whilst the father casually generated a conversation disclosing that he'd always thought the client had autism. The father explained that the mother was still upset but that the client wanted to continue the sessions. We ended the conversation and he left. The client was deeply apologetic for their mother's behaviour but was resolute in their desire to continue therapy. We discussed the prospect of autism, and the client disclosed significant information about their views and beliefs. For several years they had thought they were autistic but were too ashamed to discuss it, especially at home with their parents. We agreed to be mindful of autism but would still focus on strategies to help tackle anxiety. The therapeutic relationship strengthened, and the client disclosed additional issues about gender and sexuality (although these were not discussed with the parents). On the morning of session 11, I received an email from the client's mother. The email was lengthy and very apologetic about the behaviour in session six. The mother noted that on reflection, it was clear to her that there was an overwhelming likelihood that the client was autistic and that deep down, she knew but had avoided it because of her fears. The mother noted they had arranged an assessment via their health insurer and had used my previous email as the basis for the referral.

I was happy for the client that they would now be assessed for autism. I was pleased that the client's mother had taken her time to reflect on the situation and provide such positive comments about the therapeutic process and the benefits the client gained.

I worked with the client for 23 sessions, during which we formed a solid, trusting alliance. Things could have ended very differently had the parents decided to stop therapy. Whilst this situation does not reflect a direct issue with a client, it highlights the issues of working with a child and the parental impact. When it was clear the client was likely autistic, it felt right to disclose and discuss this with the client's parents. I had not accounted for how angry the parents might have been, but I still believe it was the right decision. Before completing therapy, the client received a formal diagnosis of autism. Whilst it has been several years since the work ended, the client has regularly dropped me communications about positive changes in their life, and with them just about to start university, their diagnosis will help to ensure that they gain the proper levels of support to achieve their potential.

Three key takeaways from this experience

1. **The importance of engaging clients in the therapy process:**
Engaging clients in the therapy process is fundamental to the success of treatment. Active participation fosters a sense of ownership and empowerment, allowing clients to invest in their own healing and growth. It enhances the therapeutic alliance, building trust and collaboration between therapist and client. This engagement facilitates tailoring interventions to the individual, ensuring relevance and applicability. In CBT, for example, the client's active role in identifying and challenging thoughts and behaviours is essential. Without engagement, the therapy process can become one-sided and less effective, lacking the vital connection that drives meaningful change and personal development.

2. **The need to establish a strong therapeutic rapport:**
Establishing a strong therapeutic rapport is a cornerstone of effective therapy. It creates a trusting and secure environment, enabling clients to feel understood, respected, and safe in sharing their thoughts and feelings. This connection encourages open communication, enhancing the collaboration between therapist and client. A strong rapport fosters client motivation and engagement in the therapeutic process, making it more likely that they will actively participate and invest in their own healing. Therapy can become rigid and superficial without this foundational relationship, impeding genuine insight and meaningful change. A robust therapeutic rapport is vital for facilitating a productive and transformative therapeutic experience.

3. **The significance of empowering clients to regain agency and control:** Empowering clients to regain agency and control is integral to therapeutic success. It enables individuals to take charge of their lives, make informed decisions and act confidently. By focusing on their strengths and abilities, clients

can move away from feelings of helplessness or dependency, fostering self-reliance and resilience. This empowerment facilitates personal growth and self-discovery, allowing clients to navigate challenges more effectively. Ultimately, regaining agency and control enhances immediate therapeutic outcomes and equips individuals with the skills and mindset needed for ongoing well-being and fulfilment.

What was the most challenging aspect of this experience?

The most challenging aspect was how to raise the suggestion of an autism assessment, specifically given the reaction from the client';s mother. The resistance and anger expressed by the mother created a highly tense situation, putting both the therapist and the client in an uncomfortable and complex position. The challenge here lay in navigating the mother's immediate emotional response and maintaining the integrity of the therapeutic process, supporting the client's needs, and ultimately leading to the appropriate assessment. This situation required delicate handling, ethical consideration, and clear communication; all while managing intense emotional reactions and maintaining the trust and progress made in therapy. It underscores the intricacy of working with young people and the multifaceted relationships that therapy with young clients can entail.

How did this experience help you improve your practice?

This experience has helped me improve my CBT practice by deepening my understanding of the complex dynamics of working with young people and their families. It has sharpened my skills in handling unexpected and intense emotional reactions, particularly when broaching sensitive subjects like a potential autism diagnosis. Furthermore, it has highlighted the importance of clear communication, ethical transparency and maintaining client trust, even in challenging circumstances. By navigating this difficult situation successfully, I have demonstrated resilience and adaptability in my therapeutic approach, likely enhancing my ability to support clients and their families in the future.

What key things have you implemented in your practice?

The key things I have implemented in my practice include a robust approach to building and maintaining rapport, careful formulation and assessment of underlying conditions, and a commitment to ethical transparency with both clients and their families. Additionally, my handling of the situation demonstrated a thoughtful approach to client empowerment and a focus on individualised therapy that considers not just symptoms but the broader context of the client's life, including sensory issues and family dynamics. These aspects reflect a comprehensive and compassionate approach to therapy that prioritises the client's well-being and personal growth. A thorough assessment process and ongoing formulation underpin all of this.

How did clinical supervision support you through the experience? Did you access any additional supports?

My supervisor played an essential role in supporting me through this challenging experience. They acted as a valuable sounding board, allowing me to explore my rationale and processes and identify areas for growth and development.

My five key takeaway points from supervision:

- **Listening and reflecting:** My supervisor's willingness to listen and reflect back to me provided a critical space for introspection and self-awareness. This interaction facilitated a deeper understanding of my thoughts and feelings about the situation, which may have led to more informed |decision-making.
- **Exploring growth and development:** Through supervision, I was able to not just react to the situation but actively seek opportunities to learn and grow from it. By focusing on areas of growth and development, I shifted the focus from merely

resolving the problem to enhancing my overall professional practice.

- **Enhancing confidence:** My supervisor's support has played a vital role in building my confidence. Facing a difficult situation can be unnerving, and having someone to guide and affirm my decisions likely made a significant difference in my ability to navigate the challenges.

- **Ensuring adherence to professional and ethical boundaries:** The complex nature of the situation required careful consideration of professional and ethical boundaries. My supervisor's guidance in this area ensured that I was acting in accordance with the client's best interests, maintaining the integrity of my practice, and complying with professional standards.

- **Potential additional support:** My supervision approach also represents a commitment to continuous professional development. Engaging in this reflective practice with my supervisor could imply an openness to accessing additional support, such as further training or consultation with experts if needed, to ensure the best outcomes for my clients.

In summary, the support from my supervisor was multi dimensional, contributing to my immediate handling of the situation and my ongoing professional development. This relationship was instrumental in guiding me through a challenging experience, reinforcing my confidence and competence as a CBT psychotherapist.

What would you have done differently?

With the benefit of hindsight, some aspects of the situation might have been approached differently. One element that resonates with me is the client's body language when his mother displayed signs of annoyance and anger. While I would have preferred to prevent this reaction from occurring in the client's presence, it would not have been appropriate to request the client to leave the room (my trying to protect the client was discussed in depth during supervision).

Moreover, it might have been prudent to prepare additional information on autism for the session, ensuring it was readily accessible to address any questions or concerns. Having a copy of my assessment and formulation immediately available for the client's mother could have alleviated some of her distress and provided clarity.

Apart from these considerations, I am confident in the decisions made and do not believe that substantial alterations to my approach would have been warranted.

What guidance and learning would you offer other professionals?

All therapy is inherently individual and unique, reflecting each client's distinct needs, experiences, and circumstances. This variability can make it challenging to offer clear-cut guidance and learning that applies universally. Nevertheless, certain foundational principles hold across the therapeutic landscape. The importance of good quality, balanced supervision cannot be overstated. Such supervision provides a supportive environment for reflection and growth, which helps increase confidence and professionalism. Adherence to an ethical framework ensures that practice remains principled and client-focused. Effective communication fosters trust and understanding within the therapeutic relationship and with other stakeholders. Regular Continuing Professional Development (CPD) ensures therapists stay abreast of the latest research, techniques, and best practices, allowing them to adapt and respond to the individual nuances of each therapeutic relationship. These core elements collectively contribute to a robust, responsive and responsible approach to the diverse and complex therapy world.

Below are seven significant points to help offer additional guidance:

1. **Open communication and ethical transparency**

   a.**Guidance:** Always strive for honest communication with clients and their families. If a potential underlying condition becomes apparent, discuss it openly and ethically.

   b.**Learning:** Transparency fosters trust and may lead to unexpected reactions. Being prepared to manage a range of emotional responses is crucial.

2. **Emotional regulation and professional composure:**

   a.**Guidance:** Remain composed, even in the face of strong emotions from clients or their families. Your calm demeanour can help de-escalate tense situations.

   b.**Learning:** Emotional self-awareness and self-care strategies are essential for maintaining professional objectivity and empathy.

3. **Collaboration with families:**

   a.**Guidance:** Recognise the importance of family dynamics and work collaboratively with parents and guardians. Understand that their perspectives may differ, and that's okay, but confidentiality must always be observed.

   b.**Learning:** Respectful dialogue and careful listening can transform resistance into cooperation. Give space for parents to process information at their own pace.

4. **Cultural and individual Sensitivity:**

   a.**Guidance:** Acknowledge and respond to individual differences and cultural considerations. This includes understanding a parent's profession or personal beliefs that might affect their perception.

   b.**Learning:** Build a therapeutic alliance by being mindful of individual needs and backgrounds, including potentially sensitive topics like gender, sexuality, or disability.

5. **Evidence-based assessment and intervention:**

   a. **Guidance:** Use a formulation-driven approach, informed by evidence, to assess and plan interventions. This can guide your therapy, even in complex or ambiguous situations.

b. Learning: Ongoing assessment and adjustment to therapeutic strategies, grounded in evidence-based practice, will support positive outcomes.

6. **Informed consent and boundaries:**

   a. Guidance: Establish clear boundaries and obtain informed consent from both the child and the parents (where necessary). This includes discussing potential further diagnostic assessments and therapy goals.

   b. Learning: Transparency about roles and expectations at the outset can prevent misunderstandings later on.

7. **Reflection and supervision:**

   a. Guidance: Engage in regular self-reflection and seek supervision when needed. Complex cases require careful consideration and sometimes an external perspective.

   b. Learning: Reflective practice and professional supervision enhance growth, accountability, and resilience in challenging situations.

In summary, my experience provides valuable lessons for professionals in building open communication, maintaining professional composure, understanding individual and family dynamics, employing evidence-based practices, and nurturing long-term relationships. These insights are applicable across various therapeutic contexts and can contribute to more effective, empathetic, and ethical practice.

Chapter Six

Power, Sexuality & Inexperience:
Lessons from a Student Counsellor

Caroline O'Grady

I am a person-centered psychotherapist and clinical supervisor with over 17 years of experience in the mental health sector. I hold an honours degree in psychology and a postgraduate diploma in person-centred therapy. Throughout my professional journey, I have continually engaged in further training to support and enhance my practice, including trauma-focused approaches such as the Cognitive Resource Model.

My career has allowed me to support clients across diverse areas, including:
- Specialist inpatient adolescent mental health services
- Sexual health services, including work around sexual abuse and trauma
- Supporting clients who are questioning their gender identity
- School-based settings

Currently, I manage a large team of counsellors working within high school settings, providing essential mental health support to students.

I am deeply passionate about early intervention for young people and adults, and I am committed to promoting mental well-being at the earliest possible stage. Additionally, I take great pride in mentoring and supporting newly qualified counsellors as they find their footing in this rewarding profession.

"You're a newly qualified counsellor, unleashed into the world, apron strings have been sharply cut. The anticipation, the visceral fear. You know what to do Caroline. You've got to know. It's go time."

Setting the scene

It's January in Scotland; the ground is icy and the air is crisp. I make my way to one of my placements. The visceral mix of excitement, anxiety and energy for the day ahead is ever present. I recognise the feeling well now. I open the creaky door and my day begins.

As students, we are taught the theory. We are guided by the greats before us, the mantra of 'trust the process' rings loudly in my ear. Carl Rogers taught us that the clients you see, they are the experts - not you. The client has the innate ability to self-actualise. (Rogers, 1957).

That process is within them. Your job is not to reach in and find it before them, but rather sit side by side with them as they discover it themselves. My course tutors, supervisors and peers supported this concept, "Do not try and fix Caroline, fixing is not your job here."

I took my time to consider where I wanted to gain my client hours. My previous experience had mainly been focused on young people in psychiatry. I felt comfortable with young people, and I felt comfort in the medical model. I needed to challenge myself to move away from a medical concept to life through a person-centred lens. My course required my client hours to be completed with 70 per cent adults, so it seemed pragmatic to find a placement which was adult based. I questioned my options and interests. I also questioned where I could access this in a timely manner to meet the requirements of my course. As students, we recognise this is an important consideration. As qualified therapists, course leaders and supervisors it is also important to recognise the dynamic within this, the student will naturally be in a position of inequality.

It did not take me much time to find a placement that worked for me, my course and my life. It was a mental health service where my client base would be predominantly but not exclusively women. I supported mums who were heavily pregnant, mums who had very recently given birth, and mums whose babies were no longer with them. As a mum myself, I didn't shy away from the processes they brought. The pain, the anguish, the grief, the loss and the joy. Somehow, I felt comfort and grateful in being the one that could walk alongside them. I will forever have gratitude and awe for all those clients who trusted me in their journey.

As a student I was challenged. I leafed through my notes when I wasn't sure, I referred to the course reading list, I sought support where I could. Yet still, I did not always find the 'answer.' I practiced the skills I was taught. I reflected back. I held the silence. I paraphrased. Yet at times; nothing. Why weren't the things I was being taught working? Then came the panic. But I was still learning; and I see that now. My supervisor held this well for me. She soothed me in times of uncertainty, and she held the space for me when I had to ask myself, "What am I doing wrong?" We worked well together. We met every two weeks and reflected. She slowly but surely helped my confidence to increase.

The client

It was all going so well, until it wasn't. Like a core memory, this image is ingrained in my mind and soul.

I have been assigned a new client. I am handed the client's information minutes before I meet them. I compose myself as always, take my three belly breaths, adjust my dress and fix my hair. I open the door to the waiting room. I look at my sheet. This cannot be right. "David" I say and scan the waiting room. The silence is only broken by the trickling of the leaking water fountain. A man makes eye contact with me. I try, most likely unsuccessfully, to hide the wave of panic which I feel from my toes to my head. "David?" I ask tentatively. As he stands, he towers over my 5-foot frame, shakes my hand and introduces himself.

I was expecting the client to be a woman - a mum – however, here was David.

The room

As counsellors, I believe we can all cast our minds back to our own experiences of therapy rooms best described as cupboards! Windowless, soulless spaces at times become our counselling homes. As adaptable, resilient practitioners - we always make it work, we flourish in the darkness!

I want to paint you a picture and take you on this journey with me. As a student I was grateful for the placement, I did not feel I was in the position to advocate for myself in respect of the room. And in turn, the client either. It was a running joke within my peer groups that students were given the worst rooms.

David and I made our way along the corridor, to the last room in the building. The corridor lit by the flickering of the 'Fire Exit' sign, accompanied by the musty dampness. I smiled as I showed him into the room.

"You are wondering why I'm here aren't you?" he asked. I most certainly was. A man in a service accessed by women - I had not been prepped for this. My person-centred gurus hadn't versed me on this. I felt unprepared. I felt shaken. I felt powerless. I felt something I didn't have a name for. I didn't have a theory yet that explained it. I hadn't reached this part of the course. Retrospectively, I can now give this a name, a concept, a label - yes sometime person-centered therapists can mention labels!

Here in this very room, in real life, was a power dynamic. Rogers told me (professionally) "you don't hold the power - the client does." However, this concept as a student confused me. How can I hold no power when they come to see me? They want me to help them. I must have some power. I told myself, "Push that thought down Caroline."

However, this time the power dynmic was clear from that first eye contact. He held it, and he liked it.

The sessions initially began light, I worked very hard to provide those core conditions, (which are empathy, unconditional positive regard, and congruence (authenticity). These conditions create a safe and trusting therapeutic environment, allowing clients to explore their thoughts and feelings openly, fostering personal growth and self-understanding). Something I always felt came naturally to me before my training, yet they raced through my head now as the 'must dos'! I showed empathy with my head tilts, my reflections of how difficult things felt for him. I worked with him without judgement as he guided our sessions. We worked for a few weeks on what he brought to sessions, his relationships, his work, his life with his children. He spoke often of not being listened to at home, of seeking validation elsewhere, looking for comfort away from home. What I can reflect on now, is that I was sitting with a lost man. His world had drastically changed, and it wasn't just him and his wife anymore. Something I could understand as a mum myself. I recognised the shift that comes when your children are born. I see this in him, when I look hard, I witness loneliness.

I won't go into everything we worked on in sessions. What I will do is give you insight into our sessions through one situation that occurred. Feeling unwell, I had to suggest to him that we end the session early, due to me beginning to feel very unwell. This was visible in the room. When I raised the possibility of ending the session early, I was met with:

"No, we won't be ending early, I have made my way all the way here for this session."

Retrospectively, I should not have gone to placement feeling unwell, however, I did. I was a student that couldn't afford to miss sessions. I also had a misguided logic at that time, that I would let everyone down if I was not there – I questioned my own conditions of worth. Retrospectively, I would have used a statement, and not a question. But that's not what I did. This is one insight into a slowly developing power shift in the room.

So, I carried on, we continued the session - me unwell, the client continuing in the process. He thanked me at the end for continuing as I walked him up the stairs and out of the building.

What about that other core condition? What about congruence? I tried. I did. I reflected on this being a difficult condition to offer to him at that time. However, I sat with what he was bringing, I tried not to, but I couldn't relate to him. I wasn't in his world, and I couldn't get in. Experience now tells me we were never in psychological contact. I wasn't able to be authentic.

My lack of experience and fear meant I couldn't name what was happening in the room. I noticed the changes as the weeks went on. The way he moved the chair closer to mine, the emphasis on asking me how I was? How my weekend was? The change in body language. I see it all now, clearly. I feel it in my gut.

Then it happened. David arrived with a 'shifty' demeanour that morning. He was preoccupied, uneasy. His appearance was no different. He always came dressed in a suit. The smell of aftershave overtook the room.

"I have sexual feelings for you."

Time stood still. He leant back in his chair, arms crossed over his body and let me sit with the information. Silence.

Now, as an experienced counsellor and supervisor, I can confidently tell you how I would manage this situation. With confidence, with knowledge, and standing in my power. I might use silence; I might be curious to understand why he mentioned this now? I might wonder about the possibility of counter transference. I know now what I would do, I would excitedly unpack what could have been a breakthrough in our therapeutic relationship. I might reflect back to him that he tells me his wife 'doesn't listen' their sex life was 'boring' I would name this shift in power as I see it now. I would lean into myself to congruently offer unconditional positive regard to a man, who in effect was describing loneliness. A need for connection and validation. A man, that like a woman in the service, just needed support.

What did I do? As a student with less than a year of client hours I panicked. I froze. I can take personal responsibility for freeze being my reaction to fear. I hold onto that as my own.

I scanned my brain for what my course taught me about sexuality in the counselling room.

What did the BACP say? They told me,

We will not have sexual relationships with or behave sexually towards our clients, supervisees or trainees.

I knew that the BACP said don't have sexual relationships or behave sexually as the therapist. But what if it's the client? The client was behaving sexually to me. I am skilled and well versed at self-reflection; I own what is my own. A background in psychology, and life experience has equipped me to separate what is mine and what is someone else's. I knew what I felt. I felt fear. I felt unequipped. I responded in the only way I knew how at that time.

"I will have to ask my placement supervisor about what to do about this."

"That's what to do, Caroline," was the response I was met with. What followed was 40 minutes of incongruent, surface level conversation. I can't claim for it to have been therapy, it wasn't. We ended the session agreeing that he would come back for his next session, and I would let him know the decision my supervisor would make - I wasn't making the decision, was I?

"Supervisors are expected to own their power and use it as a force for good, but powerful roles can be played badly."
Van, Ooijen (2015)

As a therapist, I believe one of our greatest assets is our ability for self-reflection. For myself, I achieve this through supervision. We sit with it in the room with the client, with congruence of course. But then, we take it to our supervisor. For contemplation, reflection, answers! I have been very lucky within my counselling journey that my external supervisors have been experienced, holding and wonderful. Those supervisors have helped me immensely along the way.

The response from my supervisor:
"Oh, you will keep working with him!"

In anticipation, I sat awaiting the service lead. My mind racing at the thought of having to approach the 'big boss' recognising my place as a trainee, asking for help. Asking essentially to be held. I relayed the series of events that led to this meeting. I was asked to give a synopsis of the work - what had I done to help the client so far? What had we worked on so far? It felt as though there was an undertone of 'this is on you Caroline to have done a good job so far, so tell me.'

At this point it's important to consider there is a difference in preferred modalities between myself and the service manager. Our ways of working were different, and the difference in our levels of experience were vast, which played significantly into this relationship dynamic. My placement supervisor had been a counsellor for decades, and I was in awe of their expertise and was eager to listen (and be rescued). Unfortunately, what I was met with was more questions, an undertone of judgements and suggestions to lean into the sexual dynamic that presented itself to me in the room. The suggestions of understanding the client's sexual relationship with his wife, then transference towards me and the excitement of being able to challenge this client on his sex life and relationship, felt palpable from the manager. I sat, in quiet disbelief. I reflected that not only were they not going to hear my concerns and accept my lack of experience and fear, they also expected me to do some fantastic work with this man and have outcomes that would be dynamic and exciting. I left the room, deflated and despondent.

What followed were another six sessions with this man. In truth - years later - I cannot tell you what we worked on, or what he took from the sessions. What played out for me was a trauma response. My mind trying to protect me, most likely dissociated from what happened after that. One thing I can be certain of, I shouldn't have been expected to continue in that same room, in that same situation.

I don't write this from a place of blame, in fact I write this as an example of what can go wrong when we do not address power, sexuality and inexperience. At different points in my practice, I have felt that maybe the right thing was not to rescue me as a student in that situation, it gave me a learning opportunity. It taught me how to manage a situation that many other students in my course had not yet been met with. I learnt a lot. I feel it's important not to consider one single point of blame here. It's not - it's a series of cries for help.

Here's what should happen:

1. Psychological contact between counsellor and client.
2. The client is incongruent (anxious or vulnerable).
3. The counsellor is congruent.
4. The counsellor shows unconditional positive regard towards the client.
5. The client receives empathy from the counsellor.
6. The client perceives acceptance and unconditional positive regard.

Tudor and Merry, 2006: 23-24

Rogers spoke often of his six necessary conditions for change. When I reflect, not only on myself, but also on the client, which of these can I say, with certainty, were felt in the room? From my training and before, I know I can offer the three core conditions naturally.

However, in this circumstance - congruence was on a shaky ledge. Was he in psychological contact? I can't say for certain. I felt connection, I felt he had a space to air his fears and inner thoughts. Was it deep visceral work? Again, I don't know. I never will.

What I do know is that if the counsellor - trainee or not - does not feel safe, grounded and confident, the work will feel more difficult. We require psychological and physical safety. We speak about the space in counselling often, we advocate for ourselves and our clients. We know the importance of the environment and how that creates a gateway to connection. And yet, as students we are not always afforded that consideration. We need to do better, as practitioners, but also as a wider group of therapists and organisations to hear our students when they say "help me to feel safe."

The voice of the supervisor

Many years have passed and I am now a supervisor. I will now change the viewpoint of this scenario and respond as the supervisor of the student counsellor. Stay with me!

My supervisee in training comes to me for supervision. They describe a series of difficult events. They are new to counselling - not totally inexperienced practitioners - however they are new to the counselling profession. They are asking for guidance, looking for answers - a way out maybe? They want me to tell them they don't need to work with the client anymore. In reality, they want to be rescued. I say that without judgement and with empathy. This can be the place of being a student counsellor. They are learning, but they need an element of being held.

What would I have done, knowing what I know now? I believe I would have picked up on the cues. I would have listened to what they were saying - both with words and with actions. I could have held the space for them to hear what was going on. I could have asked, "why don't you feel safe and how can we create an environment where you do?" I might spend some time tapping into the fear, "where is that fear in your body and how do you know what it is?"

I also might consider facilitating a conversation between the student, the placement and the training provider to create some clarity and space to allow the student to feel heard.

I also might have asked, "What do you need from me?"

Let's talk about sex (or not).

I reflect on this experience to share the lessons I've learned and the insights gained, telling a story I wish someone could have shared with me. To do so, I must embrace vulnerability and ask myself some important questions. I mentioned that the client told me he had sexual feelings for me. What were my feelings? At the time, I was in my early 20s, single, and, though I find it uncomfortable to describe my appearance—largely because it's irrelevant—I would say I was not unattractive. I share my single status only for context. At that stage in my personal life, I was not seeking or interested in physical or sexual relationships—a topic for another chapter. My counselling training was a significant focus for me, taking up much of my life alongside raising my young children.

This client could be described as handsome. He consistently presented the best version of himself, arriving each week in a suit and carrying a notable presence. In a different context, I can acknowledge that there might have been the potential for physical attraction. However, this acknowledgment did not influence my actions or decisions with the client. After all, as we know, power dynamics in therapy are not solely tied to sexual attraction.

So, what now?

I can honestly tell you that this situation massively shaped the therapist, supervisor and woman I am today. I stand in my power now because I feel it, I know it's there and I know how to advocate for myself and my clients.

As a supervisor and manager, it informs my decision making and my process. I am more in tune with the unsaid now. Power dynamics have always fascinated me, when you add in sexuality and gender - you have me sold!

I have great belief and confidence in our person-centred colleagues who paved the way for us. They guide us to lean into those core conditions, the importance of the relationship in the conduit of change.

I share this with you in the hope that when you read this, I hope you cannot relate! I hope you are supported by your peers and supervisors and course leaders. I hope this makes you pause and ask yourself,' "What happens when therapy goes wrong when you are a student?"

Three key takeaways from this experience:
1. **The importance of psychological safety**: This experience highlighted the critical need for both physical and psychological safety in the therapeutic environment. Feeling unsafe or unsupported can significantly hinder the therapeutic process for both the client and the therapist.
2. **Navigating power dynamics:** The encounter with David underscored the complex nature of power dynamics in the therapeutic relationship. It illustrated how these dynamics can shift and impact the therapy, emphasising the necessity

for therapists to recognise and address them appropriately.

3. **Value of effective supervision:** The pivotal role of supervision in providing support, guidance, and a reflective space for therapists, especially those in training, was made evident. The lack of adequate supervisory support in this instance highlighted the need for supervisors to be attuned to the needs and concerns of their supervisees.

How did this experience help you improve your practice?

This challenging experience profoundly impacted my development as a therapist. It:

- **Enhanced self-awareness:** Forced me to confront my limitations, fears, and the areas where I needed growth, particularly in handling power dynamics and sexual transference.
- **Improved client management skills:** Taught me to handle difficult situations with more confidence and skill, and to set clear boundaries with clients.
- **Reinforced the need for safety:** Cemented my understanding of the importance of creating a safe therapeutic space, both physically and psychologically, for my clients and myself.

How did clinical supervision support you through the experience? Did you access any additional supports?

Supervision played a crucial, albeit initially inadequate, role in my navigation of this experience. Initially, the lack of supportive supervision left me feeling unsupported and unprepared. However, reflecting on this:

- **Initial supervision challenges:** The supervisory response I received failed to provide the necessary support, highlighting the importance of having a responsive and understanding supervisor.

- **Seeking additional support:** I learnt to seek additional support from peers, other mentors and later, more experienced supervisors who could provide the empathy, guidance, and reflection I needed.
- **Growth in supervisory relationships:** This experience has made me more attuned to the needs of supervisees in my own practice, ensuring I provide the support I lacked.

What insights have you gained from being curious about the experience and from the process of self-reflection?

- **Importance of reflective practice:** Regular self-reflection helped me process the experience, understand my reactions, and identify areas for growth.
- **Understanding of power dynamics:** I gained a deeper insight into how power dynamics play out in therapy and the importance of addressing them explicitly when necessary.
- **Recognition of personal triggers:** Identifying my triggers and responses to fear and powerlessness has enabled me to better manage similar situations in the future.

What guidance and learning would you offer other professionals?

- **Prioritise safety:** Ensure both physical and psychological safety in the therapeutic environment. Advocate for yourself and your clients if the environment is inadequate.
- **Seek supervision:** Find a supervisor who provides the necessary support, guidance, and reflective space. Don't hesitate to seek additional support if your needs aren't being met.
- **Be aware of power dynamics:** Understand that power dynamics can shift and significantly impact the therapeutic relationship. Be prepared to recognise and address these dynamics appropriately.
- **Engage in reflective practice:** Regular self-reflection is crucial

for growth and understanding. Use it to process experiences, understand your reactions, and identify areas for improvement.

- **Advocate for yourself:** As a student or a professional, it's important to advocate for your needs and boundaries. If something feels unsafe or inappropriate, speak up and seek the necessary support.

By sharing these insights and guidance, I hope to help others navigate the complexities of the therapeutic journey with greater confidence and support.

References

Rogers, C. R. (1957). The necessary and sufficient conditions of therapeutic personality change. *Journal of consulting psychology,* 21(2), 95.

Tudor K and Merry T (2006) Dictionary of Person-Centred Psychology, PCCS Books

Van Ooijen E. When supervision goes wrong. Therapy Today 2015; 26(9): 32–34

https://www.linkedin.com/in/caroline-ogrady-81159a159?lipi=u rn%3Ali%3Apage%3Ad_flagship3_profile_view_base_contact_ details%3 B5U0H7tNjSrm6B%2BxW9axtUw%3D%3D

Chapter Seven

Rage Unleashed: Narcissistic Challenges and Lessons Learnt

Lee Paterson

I am an integrative therapist and set up my private practice in January 2020 in South Lanarkshire, Scotland. Prior to the COVID-19 pandemic, my sessions were all face to face, however, like most therapists I transitioned to video and telephone appointments throughout lockdown. Post-lockdown, my practice very quickly returned to face to face.

In conjunction with my private practice, I have also worked in a charity supporting adults and children who have experienced childhood sexual abuse. This is where I really began to comprehend the magnitude of trauma and the impact it has, not only on the person directly affected, but the ripple effect on others and society overall. Working in the field of trauma appears to be a continual learning experience, and one which I wholeheartedly embrace.

In 2019 I gained my degree in Applied Social Science in Counselling from the Jenson Newman Institute in Sydney, Australia, where I resided for almost 13 years. Prior to graduating, I worked mainly in corporate environments, however, as time passed I began to question my career choice and acknowledged my lack of job satisfaction.

I wanted to do something with purpose, something that created positive change and helped people. I reflected on challenges with my own mental health in my youth, and the prospect of what could have been different if I had accessed professional support. I couldn't help but wonder, and with that I began researching counselling courses.

I knew at this stage, a career change was imminent and, at the age of 37 - although I remained in employment - commenced my part-time study. For the first time in years, I felt excited and motivated. I'll never forget my first subject 'introduction to psychology,' my lecturer Doreen Patenall was an inspiration. She was engaging, educational and hilarious. I was hooked, and knew I made the right decision.

Approximately one year into my practice (which was still during lockdown) I was operating mainly remotely, then face to face when government restrictions allowed. I received a new client enquiry:

Peter (not his real name), was a 52-year-old male. During the telephone consultation he outlined what he hoped to gain from the process, indicating his main focus was on exploring his emotions and working on his sense of self. Recently he had begun to question who he was and his purpose. He also added that he had been in therapy a few times, but it hadn't worked out for him. He continued to explain that he also wanted to talk about his relationship with his partner Fiona (again, not her real name) with whom he'd lived for the past two years.

I outlined the contracting process and the options available and we agreed to fortnightly video appointments. The contract was signed and returned, we were ready to begin.

In the first session Peter presented on the video as relaxed and eager to talk. So much so it was difficult to get a word in! Any attempt to clarify or seek a deeper understanding resulted in him speaking over me, and he wouldn't allow me the opportunity to finish my questions. He did this in such a hurried and rushed manner, it appeared to be very dismissive, and I was quickly becoming aware of my own frustration around this.

He continued to explain there had been a couple of historical incidents of violence between himself and his partner Fiona – the police had also been involved on one occasion. Peter admitted he could get angry at times and this was something he wanted to understand more in-depth. He also advised he had a history with drug and alcohol abuse, however, this was no longer an issue.

Throughout Peter's second session, I began to identify traits of narcissism and delusions of grandeur; he delighted in telling me of his career in sales and how amazingly he performed and how his senior managers idolised him. He described his peers as 'jealous' - he was after all 'the best' within the team and the one to beat. Peter was smiling and happy to share these memories, his body language was open and the dialogue slow and steady. Given Peter was unemployed I was curious to learn more about his career and what had led to his current situation. Again, any attempt to interject and clarify were glossed over. I was beginning to anticipate such a response from Peter, as the pattern of shutting me down had become obvious and predictable.

My attempts to gently bring Peter back and refocus were also becoming tiring. I noticed signs of contempt when these self-aggrandising monologues were interrupted. His lips would tighten in the corner and his tone would change from slow and steady to quick and short. For example, when asked if we can focus on his goals, he would reply "yup," and shift uncomfortably around in his chair. Albeit, on the surface he appeared to be verbally agreeing with me, his body language and micro emotions told me otherwise.

I was also becoming aware of my hesitation on various occasions to interrupt him and my personal discomfort was becoming evident. I recognised my reluctance to upset Peter, and became aware I was 'walking on eggshells.' I began to realise that Peter wanted to control the sessions and I was enabling it.

On our third session, Peter started off by telling me about an incident a few days prior, where there had been a physical altercation with his partner Fiona. He explained that an argument had escalated, and she was pointing in his face, he pushed her away and she fell onto the kitchen floor. Fiona hurt her head and one of her limbs; she ultimately attended casualty to have it checked. After being assessed she was given the all clear and sent home to rest.

In Peter-style, attempting to minimise the seriousness of the situation yet again glossed over this admission, describing it as "just an accident", claiming it was all very silly and they made up straight away. It was very apparent there was no accountability for his part in this, or any sense of remorse for what happened to Fiona and the harm he inflicted on her. I interrupted him, again mindful to do this with a gentle tone given his previous reactions. I informed him that based on this disclosure I would not be able to continue working with him unless we contracted into our agreement that there would be no further violence between them.

Peter looked taken aback, and the reaction which followed can only be described as 'zero to one hundred.' It was beyond anger, it was rage. Peter began screaming and yelling at me, stating I had no right to tell him what to do, and how fed up he was of everyone doing this to him. His face was red and angry, I watched as he spewed out a dialogue of hate and profanities.

In that moment, the shock set in, and my inner narrative was screaming one word 'wow' over and over on repeat. I was stunned and had to continually remind myself to breathe and stay composed. Following this, a dialogue of panic began running through my mind in an attempt to find a solution to what was unfolding in front of me.

At this point he got out of his chair and forced his face towards the camera, his lips tight, his teeth visibly more prominent, and saliva foaming from his mouth. His eyes were wide and black, swearing and screaming at me, words that I couldn't retain. He pointed his finger into the camera unleashing his rage.

In the bottom right-hand corner of my screen where my camera was reflecting back at me. I could see a face, a calm composed person watching this all unfold. There was a brief moment in time before I realised it was me. It was like watching someone else's reaction as my internal response did not seem to be in sync with my cool and calm exterior.

In an attempt to ground Peter and diffuse the situation, I invited him to join me in a breathing exercise, I spoke slowly and deliberately in the hope he would replicate my pace. It was like a switch went on and with that he stopped screaming, he started to mirror me and joined in, his comeback was as quick and surprising as the escalation itself. Albeit, I could see his eyes remained wide and starey, I felt reassured I had handled this well and, I could feel myself finally catching a breath. I continually repeated myself, mindful of maintaining my slow and calm tone. I could feel the relief begin to wave over me as he slowly sat back in his chair.

As he did this, he began to regurgitate quietly what had just happened and blamed me for telling him what to do. His speech quickened and before I knew it, we were right back at the start, the rage had engulfed him once again. I knew he was moments away from launching himself back out of his chair.

My response was different this time, I tried to get ahead of the reaction, with a calm tone I advised the consequences to this behaviour continuing would result in the termination of the session. My request was ignored as his anger intensified; therefore, I swiftly ended the session. With my heart racing and body full of adrenaline I paced my study trying to process what had just happened. I had never witnessed such a reaction, one which I felt was completely disproportionate to the situation. I then called my supervisor – who supported and guided me through my process.

Three key takeaways from this experience:

1. **Recognising and addressing power dynamics:** This experience underscored the importance of maintaining a balanced power dynamic in therapeutic sessions. It highlighted the need for therapists to be vigilant about clients attempting to control the sessions and the necessity of setting clear boundaries to ensure productive and respectful interactions.

2. **Handling crisis situations calmly:** The incident with Peter emphasised the critical skill of managing acute emotional crises. The ability to stay composed and utilise grounding techniques effectively can significantly impact the outcome of such volatile situations, demonstrating the importance of having a toolkit of strategies to de-escalate intense emotions.

3. **The importance of contracting and boundaries:** The necessity of clear contracting was made evident. Ensuring clients understand and agree to boundaries, particularly concerning non-violence, is crucial. This experience reinforced the need to be firm and explicit about these both the client and the therapist.

How did this experience help you improve your practice?

This experience has enhanced my awareness of the dynamics that can unfold in therapeutic sessions, particularly with clients who exhibit challenging behaviours such as narcissism or aggression. It has improved my ability to set and enforce boundaries firmly and compassionately. Additionally, it reinforced the importance of being prepared for crisis situations and having a clear action plan for such scenarios. This has led to an increased focus on crisis intervention training and the incorporation of regular boundary-setting discussions in my practice.

How did clinical supervision support you through the experience? Did you access any additional support?

Supervision played a crucial role in processing this experience. My supervisor provided a safe space to discuss the incident, offering valuable feedback and strategies for handling similar situations in the future. The support helped to normalise my reactions and emotions, alleviating feelings of isolation and self-doubt. I also accessed additional support such as peer consultations and professional development workshops focusing on managing difficult clients and trauma-informed care. These resources provided further insights and practical tools to enhance my competence and confidence in handling such cases.

What insights have you gained from being curious about the experience and from the process of self-reflection?

Self-reflection and curiosity about this experience have led to several insights. I have gained a deeper understanding of the psychological patterns and defence mechanisms employed by clients with narcissistic traits. It has also made me more aware of my own triggers and emotional responses, helping me to develop better self-regulation techniques. Furthermore, this experience has highlighted the importance of ongoing professional development and the value of seeking support and guidance from supervisors and peers.

What guidance and learning would you offer other professionals?

- **Set clear boundaries early on:** Ensure that clients understand and agree to the boundaries of the therapeutic relationship from the outset. This can prevent potential power struggles and enhance the safety and efficacy of the therapy.
- **Stay composed during crises:** Develop and practice de-escalation techniques to manage emotional crises effectively. Remaining calm and composed can significantly influence the client's ability to regain control over their emotions.
- **Utilise supervision and peer support:** Regular supervision and peer consultations are invaluable. They provide a platform for discussing challenging cases, gaining different perspectives, and receiving emotional support.
- **Engage in continuous learning:** Attend workshops, training, and professional development opportunities to stay updated on best practices for handling difficult clients and trauma-informed care.
- **Reflect and adapt:** Continuously reflect on your experiences and be open to adapting your approach. Self-reflection can lead to profound insights and personal growth, enhancing your effectiveness as a therapist.

CHAPTER EIGHT

Ten to Twenty Percent: When Therapy is not Therapeutic

Ravind Jeawon

Ravind Jeawon MIACP is an accredited, Dublin based psychotherapist and founder of Talk Therapy Dublin, a private service which aims to provide inclusive counselling support to clients experiencing distress. With a humanistic/integrative core training, Ravind's clinical experience began supporting community counselling services in Dublin providing psychotherapy and psychosocial support to communities affected by socioeconomic inequality, organised crime, and homelessness. Having spent over three years in this area Ravind moved into private practice and noticed further demand by minoritised clients looking for responsive counselling linked to issues around ethnicity, race, and the experience of migration. This encouraged an increasing interest in multiculturally responsive counselling, prompting Ravind to pursue further training in the area at the Nafsiyat Intercultural Centre in London. Ravind has expanded his work to include organisational and college training as well as the mentoring of students and newly qualified therapists from diverse backgrounds in Ireland. He has provided counselling services to the International Organization for Migration (IOM) in Ireland linked to their assisted voluntary return programme. He also has worked as a clinical supervisor for the IOM's Mental Health & Psychosocial Team (MHPSS) working with clients seeking international protection in Citywest Dublin. As a therapist Ravind continues to advocate for more inclusivity within mental health practice, particularly linked to core training and an improvement in multicultural responsiveness from caring professions when providing services to minoritised communities.

Publications

Ravind has co-written two book chapters on Multicultural Responsiveness with psychotherapist researcher and academic Daryl Mahon— in the publications *Trauma Informed Organizations (2022)* and *Evidence Based Counselling & Psychotherapy for the 21st Century practitioner* (2023), as well as an entire chapter on intercultural supervision in *Intercultural Supervision in Therapeutic Practice Dialogues, Perspectives and Reflections*, (2023) edited by Baffour Ababio who is clinical lead at the Nafsiyat Intercultural Centre in London.

A note on confidentiality:

The following chapter contains examples that are a mix of different cases of my own or ones that I have been close to. They have been adapted in terms of content to make sure the cases as presented adhere to the Irish Association of Counselling & Psychotherapy (IACP) code of ethics.

Introduction

It's good to talk, right? Over the past decade I have been repeatedly struck by the desire of people to engage in therapy, even in quite challenging circumstances, across a variety of clinical settings. And it works! Research has found psychotherapy to be a very effective intervention for some people experiencing distress, repeatedly demonstrating impressive effect sizes, from early meta-analysis on client outcomes (Smith & Glass, 1977), to more contemporary writing on the subject (Mahon, 2023). However, this significant demonstration of the efficacy of therapy also identifies a number of individuals who receive therapy and have negative, sometimes traumatic experiences. Some research has indicated that 10 percent of adult clients and 24 per cent of children and young people deteriorate during treatment (Hansen, Lambert, & Forman, 2002). Research also informs us that practitioners can be poor at identifying those who are not benefiting from care (Hannan et al., 2005; Hatfield, McCullough, Frantz, & Krieger, 2010; Walfish, McAlister, O'Donnell, & Lambert,

2012). As a clinician running a practice and providing supervision, I have interacted with clients and service enquiries who describe previous therapeutic experiences as distressing, unhelpful or even re-traumatising. Cooper (2008) mentions a figure of 80 percent of people benefiting from therapy as opposed to no treatment at all. This chapter will focus on the 10-20 percent (depending what studies you look at) who do not benefit. I will explore several adapted clinical examples from my practice to draw attention to client experiences where there have been difficulties and ethical dilemmas that have disrupted their therapy.

All names in the following case studies have been changed.

Case 1: A man alone

Alan had been working with Gabi for close to one year. They had formed a stable therapeutic relationship over this time as she began to open up about problematic relationships with men in her life while delving into a history of trauma that took place in her childhood. Gabi had started becoming more emotional in sessions as the months progressed, often appearing quite dysregulated, which had led Alan to make interventions to help ground and soothe her. One week, after a particularly intense session Gabi did not return to therapy. The next contact Alan had in relation to her was being made aware of a complaint to his accrediting body linked to inappropriate behaviour in session. Gabi described being invited to interact sexually in session and also shared concerns about the length of sessions running over and a lack of professionalism. Alan described a very different set of events and was able to cast doubt on some accusations due to having proof of payment times linked to his electronic card reader records and also phone communication records. Alan had often met Gabi alone in the building for these sessions and a lengthy investigation ensued. Alan is now considering leaving work in private practice to work in a larger organisation.

Reflections:

This example highlights the importance in supervision of attention to practitioner safety in allocation of clients and in suitability of the venue. In my own practice, I have often paid particular attention to practitioner safety when allocating certain clients/presenting issues to both cisgender female and trans/non-binary practitioners, but less so with respect to cisgender men. This points to an unconscious bias with respect to gender on my part which has influenced my behaviour. Do I bring this into my role as a supervisor? In this case example, issues of safety (both client and therapist) strike me as pertinent as well as the screening or allocation decisions that led to these two individuals working together in an isolated private practice setting. The intersecting themes of gender, trauma, ethics, privilege and power may be areas for reflection as well as the pressures of managing and working in private practice which has been described by some as a potentially lonely, isolating experience. If so, how might this play out in the therapeutic encounter? Are there particular safety concerns cisgender male practitioners need to consider in the context of work in the 21 st century?

Case 2: Maga

Sam is in his 30's seeking therapy for low mood and relationship issues with his Irish husband. He has completed a course of CBT and feels this did not get at everything and wants to try a different approach. He is the main income earner in the home and describes a background of poverty in America. He was raised by a single mum who had mental health issues which required his extended family to help out. He explains that being one of the few white kids in the neighbourhood where he grew up, meant that he shouldn't ever complain. He did not know his father. He has recently become a dad himself. He had been planning on moving back to the USA, when his daughter became seriously ill. The Irish health system provided a much more viable option for treatment cost-wise than the US alternative, changing his decision to return. He is now settled in Dublin with his daughter in school and busy in his career. He had initially presented to another counselling centre in Dublin, where the intake therapist made an "off the cuff" remark about America, "Perhaps not being made so great again" (Donald Trump had just been elected a year or so before). Feeling badly after this session he declined to go back and decided to seek out a "non Irish" therapist instead.

Reflections:

Multicultural work is moving away from the idea of cultural competency, towards cultural humility; an example of which is the multicultural orientation approach (MCO) (Watkins et al, 2019). It is built on three pillars: **cultural humility** (a way of being with diversity), **cultural opportunities** (a way of identifying and responding to cultural content in session or encounters) and cultural comfort (a way of understanding ourselves before, during and after these encounters). It also provides a way of working with microaggression when it emerges in sessions, potentially posing a significant risk of working alliance rupture (Hook et al, 2016). Microaggressions are the everyday verbal, nonverbal, and environmental slights, snubs, or insults, whether intentional or unintentional, which communicate hostile, derogatory, or negative messages to target persons based solely upon their marginalised group membership (Sue &Sue, 2016). The above case contains a microaggression which was the catalyst for the immediate cessation of therapy. Research highlights disparities in mental healthcare delivery to minoritised groups with many practitioners having better outcomes with white clients (Drinane et al., 2016; Hayes et al., 2015). However, the above example is interesting as the multi- layered cultural content occurs between a white Irish practitioner and white American born client. Ethnicity, gender, politics, socio economic issues and physical health are all relevant which invites consideration of the concept of intersectionality (Crenshaw, 1991) when working within diversity, and looks at power and privilege across a broad range of cultural variables and how this may play out in a therapeutic encounter.

Case 3: Imposter syndrome

Student practitioners beginning clinical placements often describe anxiety and concern about their judgement and ability with clients, and are in a particularly vulnerable time in their careers.

One such student was Sandra who a few months into placement was allocated a new client, Chloe. Chloe was an overwhelmed, single mum dealing with the impact of gangland activity in her life. Her children's father was in jail for manslaughter and she was concerned about his upcoming release and his increasing influence on one of her children in particular. She presented very uncomfortable in session. Sandra happened to be in her training college on the weekends and did her placement sessions on Monday afternoons. One such weekend after starting to see Chloe she had a particularly difficult skills training session with one of her classmates where she received harsh feedback on her therapeutic skills. An emphasis was made on her need to focus more on feelings within the 20-minute practice sessions. This was distressing to Sandra who was angry that the practice sessions bore little relation to the real clinical setting she worked in. That Monday she had her second session with Chloe and she was struck by an awareness that Chloe was trying very hard not to cry. With the weekend's feedback in her head she made a feelings based intervention that caused Chloe to immediately break down crying, causing her to terminate the session and walk out. Chloe never returned to therapy in the service. On reflection Sandra was furious as she knew it was too soon but was upset and wanting to prove something to herself and perhaps her trainers based on the training weekend. She often wonders what became of Chloe and her children.

Reflection:

Sandra is a new practitioner, apparently demonstrating anxiety and behaviour that would fit with being a level one practitioner using the Integrated Developmental Model (IDM) of Stoltenberg et al (1998). Safety strikes me as relevant as over a short couple of sessions, a potential lack of safety and a rupture in the educational setting, ended up re-emerging in Sandra's counselling room. Here a significant confrontation rupture to the therapeutic relationship and working alliance emerged leading to an immediate end to the process. Lots of questions come to mind, was Sandra feeling safe when she received the feedback after her skills training? Did anyone check in on her or debrief after? Did anyone consider the fact she was seeing clients on Monday? Did this lack of safety begin to emerge in these very early sessions with a vulnerable client, where a working alliance was not yet fully in place. Where would this all sit with trauma informed care of students and clients? Is there a duty of care for trainers/course supervisors to be particularly mindful of trauma informed care of both clients and students when less experienced practitioners are on placements?

Case 4: Subscribe to my channel!

Julia was 20 years old and described struggling with anxiety and panic attacks. She had completed an intake session with Rajesh, her new therapist and came out of her second session really impressed by the experience. She was excited by the new experience of opening up about how she felt and immediately took to social media to share her experience and compliment her new therapist, Rajesh. Social media was a big part of Julia's life, she shared a lot of personal information on various platforms and had a significant number of followers across them. This included sharing details on her mental health struggles often finding support and comfort from others online facing similar issues. In her third session with Rajesh, she shared how great she was finding the experience and showed him what she had posted online. This concerned Rajesh who invited Julia to revisit their contract again particularly the area around confidentiality. As they explored what had happened Rajesh shared how they had not discussed putting up content from their private sessions online. Julia explained this is how she lives her life and that she thought it might help others. Rajesh ultimately made clear that he did not believe they could work together effectively or ethically if she was to continue sharing their sessions and asked her to reconsider if she felt they were a good fit to work together. Julia was very upset and did not return to therapy, deciding to share her experiences online.

Reflection:

The advent of technology and the potential for the dehumanisation of experiences is a theme that is not new. In some cases, it may be implicitly or explicitly what drives clients to therapy. Psychotherapy now operates increasingly with clients managing the tension between their virtual and physical presence (and sense of self) and is embracing technology from video enabled remote sessions to virtual reality assisted therapy software. There are boundary issues present here as well as fertile ground for splitting or dissociative dynamics. It could also be potentially challenging in terms of safety and trauma informed care. It seems the collision of these ideas is present in the encounters between Julia and Rajesh. It raises the issue of how do we manage these contemporary issues? It also raises the issue of how do we contract confidentiality in a digital world? It also highlights the issue of how a therapist can address a situation where perceived or actual stated boundaries have been violated. Could Rajesh have leant into Julia's world more to recontract on how they could work together or discover that there was a mismatch between how they were able to contract, without blaming or shaming either of them? Was he meeting her where she was at? Are the virtual world and social media platforms an area that need more focused contracting? Consent, collaboration and communication strike me as potentially relevant words.

Case 5: "I'd actually like to talk about it"

Saoirse had been battling panic attacks and visited her GP to seek help. Her GP referred her to a psychotherapist whose approach was a manualised form of cognitive behavioural therapy (CBT) which he felt was best suited to the symptoms as described. Saoirse engaged in a structured course of six sessions of CBT with the practitioner and found it very helpful, effectively eradicating her panic attacks. She was, however, left with a niggling feeling and decided to ring a private counselling service to seek more support. Upon answering her call the practice manager, Philip, asked how they could help and Saoirse described the above story, which confused Philip, who commented that he was delighted to hear she had such a good outcome from therapy and wondered what support she now needed. Saoirse paused at this point and then quietly explained that neither the GP nor therapist had asked her what had actually happened and that she would like to talk about it. Philip gently enquired whether she would be comfortable explaining a little more to him about this and Saoirse ultimately explained that she had been raped. Upon completing a full intake on Saoirse, Philip provided a referral to one of his team experienced with working with trauma.

Reflection:

Psychotherapy seems adept at evolving new theories and formulations in order to assist people experiencing distress. The 20th century has provided hundreds of different models and the 21st century continues this trend with innovations from psychedelic assisted therapy (PAT) to virtual reality assisted therapy. Mahon (2023) outlines how outcomes research does not support the belief that a particular psychotherapy model or school can be described as superior to another and explores common factors across models that seem to be more beneficial to positive outcomes. Indeed, initial work in this area goes all the way back to Saul Rosenzweig's 1936 hypotheses that these common factors are so embedded in psychotherapy that there would be little to no difference found in the effectiveness of different approaches (Duncan, 2002). He referenced Alice in Wonderland and the dodo bird who when asked to judge a race proclaimed, "Everybody has won and all must have prizes." As practitioners, we choose specific training and are drawn to particular models. While this in itself is not a problem, does our excitement to move on to the newest therapeutic innovation or our loyalty to a particular theory ignore the basics of what we already know works across different psychotherapy interventions? The above example is interesting as the client reported a good outcome from her initial therapy experience, but perhaps the areas of collaboration and goal consensus were not quite as present as she would have liked and so she ended up going elsewhere. If she does not get the opportunity to deal with what happened, it is certainly possible that the panic attacks or other symptoms could return and that she would essentially have to undergo treatment again. So perhaps the issue worth examining here is not what therapy did wrong but to caution celebrating too early. Mature consideration of theories and approaches using a common factors approach and robust outcomes research are often ignored in core training, designed around a syllabus favouring executing therapeutic interventions based on specific theories or models. Does our core training or indeed clinical experience gradually create a preference for certain theories or models while also creating bias when considering what works or doesn't work in our approach with clients? Do we explore these issues in supervision and in therapeutic contracting and assessment?

Reflective practice:

Rather than fixate on absolutes like right or wrong, these cases are provided to prompt reflection, discussion and hopefully some constructive learning, relevant to clinical practice. I have shared some reflections below on each case myself and now hope to engage your, response, in examining these cases. This book has consistency across chapters in terms of the below questions which I now invite the reader's assistance in answering with respect to your own practice. I also invite trainers, educators and supervisors to use these questions (and the many others they may have) collaboratively with students/ trainees and supervisees where applicable.

Conclusion

The above five cases outline situations when therapy ended suddenly including one case where this was framed as a positive experience. This chapter hopes to remind practitioners, trainers, supervisors and educators to pay more attention to the '20 percent' those on our case-loads, who may be stuck, unhappy or just going with the flow. Mahon (2023) outlines how feedback informed treatment (FIT) can be adapted across modalities to help in this regard. Do we solicit feedback in our work? How often? How do we use it? Are there creative ways to do this or do we have to use software and forms in sessions? Are we modelling this in our supervisory and educational relationships? When reviewing my own work (where I have kept outcome data, so none of my student hours), my own figure stands at just over 15 percent of clients who did not benefit or left prematurely. To them I apologise for my failings as a practitioner, and it is to them I dedicate this chapter.

Three key takeaways from this experience:

1. **Prioritising client safety and collaboration:** These case examples emphasise the importance of ensuring both client and practitioner safety, particularly in therapeutic settings where power imbalances, trauma histories, or unresolved ethical dilemmas can arise. The cases highlight how a lack of safety, either physical or emotional, can lead to ruptures in the therapeutic alliance. Collaborating with clients to develop shared goals and ensuring a trauma-informed approach is critical for successful outcomes.

2. **The importance of multicultural responsiveness and humility:** The cases demonstrate the relevance of multicultural responsiveness and the need for cultural humility in therapy. Recognising and addressing microaggressions or biases, as well as understanding intersectionality in client experiences, is essential for fostering trust and therapeutic progress. Therapists should continually reflect on how cultural and personal factors may shape both the clients experience and the therapist's interventions, ensuring sensitivity to diverse backgrounds.

3. **The role of supervision and reflective practice:** Supervision played a crucial role in helping to navigate challenging

situations, as demonstrated through reflections on each case. Reflective practice, informed by supervision, allows therapists to be curious about their reactions, biases, and the dynamics of the therapeutic relationship. Supervision offers a supportive space to process emotions, refine practice, and develop insights. The experiences suggest that therapists should regularly engage in self-reflection and seek supervision to enhance their practice, particularly in complex or ethically challenging situations.

How did this experience help you improve your practice?

This experience sharpened my awareness of the complexity of the therapist-client relationship, particularly around issues of power, ethics, and cultural sensitivity. It highlighted the importance of being proactive in identifying potential ruptures in the therapeutic alliance and how crucial it is to maintain transparency, particularly when it comes to addressing sensitive issues like boundaries, confidentiality, or cultural misunderstandings. I now place greater emphasis on contracting with clients, establishing clear boundaries, and maintaining open lines of communication about their expectations and experiences.

How did supervision support you through some of these the experiences?

Supervision was invaluable during these experiences, offering both emotional support and critical feedback. It provided a safe space to process difficult emotions, validate my challenges, and reflect on my clinical decisions. I accessed peer consultation and explored literature on trauma-informed care and multicultural competence, which further expanded my ability to address similar situations in the future. This combination of supervisory support and continued learning helped me develop a more nuanced understanding of my role as a therapist.

What insights have you gained from being curious about the experience and the process of self-reflection?

Curiosity and self-reflection revealed the importance of embracing discomfort, especially when faced with ethical dilemmas or situations where cultural factors come into play. I have learnt that self-reflection is not just about reviewing client interactions but also involves exploring my own biases, assumptions, and blind spots. This process has encouraged me to adopt a more client-centred approach, ensuring that I meet clients where they are, rather than where I think they should be. It also underscored the need to keep learning, particularly in areas where therapy intersects with issues of privilege, culture, and trauma.

What guidance and learning would you offer other professionals?

1. **Emphasise client safety and boundaries:** Be proactive in establishing a safe, clear, and collaborative therapeutic environment. Ensure boundaries and goals are explicitly discussed and regularly revisited throughout the therapeutic process.

2. **Embrace cultural humility and sensitivity:** Always approach clients with cultural humility. Engage with their cultural, social, and individual identities in ways that respect and honour their experiences. Recognise and address microaggressions, even when they occur unintentionally, and continually educate yourself about multicultural responsiveness.

3. **Utilise supervision and reflective practice:** Seek out supervision consistently and use it as an opportunity to process challenging cases, emotions, and personal biases. Self-reflection is key to evolving as a therapist, and being curious about your practice will lead to greater insight and empathy for your clients.

These lessons can help fellow professionals navigate complex therapeutic dynamics and enhance the quality of care they provide to clients.

References:

Cooper, Mick (2008) *The facts are friendly*. Therapy Today, 19 (7). pp. 8-13. ISSN 1748-7846

Crenshaw, Kimberle Williams. (1991). "Mapping the Margins: Intersectionality, Identity Politics, and Violence Against Women of Color." Stanford Law Review 43(6):1241–99.

Drinane, J. M., Owen, J., & Kopta, M. (2016). Racial/ethnic disparities in psychotherapy: Does the outcome matter? Testing, Psychometrics, Methodology in Applied Psychology, 23, 531–544.

Duncan, B. L. (2002). The legacy of Saul Rosenzweig: The profundity of the dodo bird. Journal of Psychotherapy Integration, 12(1), 32–57. https://doi.org/10.1037/1053- 0479.12.1.32 Duncan, B. L. (2014). On becoming a better therapist (2nd ed.). Washing

Hannan, C., Lambert, M. J., Harmon, C., Nielsen, S. L., Smart, D. W., Shimokawa, K., & Sutton, S. W. (2005). A lab test and algorithms for identifying clients at risk for treatment failure. Journal of Clinical Psychology, 61(2), 155–163. https://doi.org/10.1002/jclp.20108

Hansen, N. B., Lambert, M. J., & Forman, E. M. (2002). The psychotherapy dose–response effect and its implications for treatment delivery services. Clinical Psychology: Science and Practice, 9(3), 329–343. https://doi.org/10.1093/clipsy.9.3.329

Hatfield, D., McCullough, L., Frantz, S. H., & Krieger, K. (2010). Do we know when our clients get worse? An investigation of therapists' ability to detect negative client change. Clinical Psychology & Psychotherapy, 17(1), 25–32. https://doi.org/10.1002/cpp.656

Hayes, J. A., Owen, J., & Bieschke, K. J. (2015). Therapist differences in symptom change with racial/ethnic minority clients. Psychotherapy, 52, 308–314.

Smith, M. L., & Glass, G. V (1977). Meta-analysis of psychotherapy outcome studies. American Psychologist, 32 , 752–760.

Hook, J. N., Farrell, J. E., Davis, D. E., DeBlaere, C., Van Tongeren, D. R., & Utsey, S. O. (2016). Cultural humility and racial microaggressions in counselling. Journal of Counselling Psychology, 63, 269–277. http://dx .doi.org/10.1037/cou0000114

Walfish, S., McAlister, B., O'Donnell, P., & Lambert, M. J. (2012). An investigation of self-assessment bias in mental health providers. Psychological Reports, 110(2), 639–644. https://doi.org/10.2466/02.07.17.PR0.110.2.639-644

Mahon, D. (2023). *Evidence Based Counselling & Psychotherapy for the 21 st Century Practitioner.* Bingley. Emerald Publishing

Stoltenberg, C. D., McNeill, B. W., & Delworth, U. (1998). Integrated developmental model for supervising counsellors and therapists. San Francisco: Jossey-Bass, Inc

Sue, D.W, Sue S, (2016). *Counselling the Culturally Diverse: Theory and Practice,* 7th ed. John Wiley

Wampold, B. E., & Imel, Z. E. (2015). *The great psychotherapy debate: The evidence for what makes psychotherapy work* (2nd ed.). Routledge/ Taylor & Francis Group.

Watkins C.E Jr, Hook J.N., Owen J, DeBlaere C, Davis D.E. and Van Tongeren, D.R. (2019) Multicultural Orientation in Psychotherapy Supervision: Cultural Humility, Cultural Comfort, and Cultural Opportunities. *American Journal of Psychotherapy*, 72 (2): 38-46

CHAPTER NINE

The One Last Job: When Curiosity and Fear Colour Therapy

Debbie Bolton

I am an accredited cognitive behavioural psychotherapist, and I have worked as a nurse in sexual health and violence for 20 years. It became apparent to me that physically attending to people's trauma was not enough. I made the decision to train as a therapist to work with the emotional trauma instead, and it has been one of the best decisions I ever made.

I have a private practice where I use a flexible approach to tailor therapy to the individual client. The modes I use are emotion focused, cognitive behavioural therapy, compassion focused, and transactional analysis. I see individuals and couples in person and on Zoom.

'The one last job'

As he walks towards the door, I find myself smiling, his frame is in proportion with the door. His capped head bows as he enters my office from the waiting room. His body moves with an exaggerated left and right movement, heavy in effect. However, when the person seated next to him is called and jumps up, my client moves as quickly and lightly as a dancer. I am curious. His reactions are sharp. I reach out my hand to introduce myself. His fingers curl and connect around my open outstretched hand. His grip is firm but not over compensatory. I respect that, and I wonder about his ego state. I suppose his size is enough of an over compensatory effect. I notice the tarnished gold sovereign rings on the fingers that are there. What happened to the other fingers?

I silently guide him with my arm towards the small cheap grey tub chair, opposite mine. My heart is beating very fast, I can feel my smile lingering. My mouth is slightly dry.

As I turn to close the door, I close my eyes and silently inhale and slowly exhale, roll my tongue around my mouth and relax my jaw, all performed in the motion of my turning to close the door. I feel particularly hyper vigilant today.

The smell in the room is of Persil washing powder. His jeans have been ironed with a fresh crisp crease down the middle. His khaki jacket has been ironed too. Ex Army? Who does this nowadays... irons jeans? Did he do this himself? He looks well cared for... by somebody else? His fisherman's hat remains firmly on his head. I can just see his eyes beneath the rim... piercing blue. His lower jaw juts forward displaying yellow and brown missing and broken teeth. I am reminded of Marlon Brando in The Godfather. His presence is palpable as is the scar across the right side of face. A delicate red brush stroke from the side of his mouth to the tip of his ear. He is sitting in the low tub chair, his knuckles an inch from the floor. The scene is almost comedic. His assessment mentions psychopathy, a term which has now been adjusted to antisocial personality disorder. I am supremely curious as to what has now brought this man to my therapy room.

I begin as I always do, explaining confidentiality and when it may be breached. I ask if he understands what I mean. He nods but I get a sense he does not understand. I explain that everything he tells me today is between me and him and that I will only speak to my supervisor or the police if there is any current criminal activity. I explain that I would never do this behind his back, and would always let him know, to support him better. This time he nods and smiles. I feel a sense of relief. I have been clear, he seems to understand this time. I feel I have set a firm boundary.

I watch as he tells me what has brought him to therapy. He wants out of gang life. He has a partner who hopes for the same.

'She's a good woman, she takes good care of me, she wants me to stop all of this... I do too.'

I ask him about the help with his stutter that he requested. He bows his head... shame? I ask him what is going on for him?

'It came on kinda suddenly, see? My niece was getting beaten up by her boyfriend, so I went down to sort him out and it was going fine,' his voice inflecting upwards, '…and I had him up against the wall my elbow at his throat, but then a couldnae get the words out, and then…' He pursed his lips and looked me fleetingly straight in the eye and then down at his feet… 'he laughed in my face.'

I sat as I watched this enormous man morph into a wee seven-year-old boy. The transformation was palpable. He lost face… this giant of a man lost face. In his world that's a crime in itself.

"So, just one more job then…"

I feel instantly triggered by his words and acutely aware I've heard these exact same words before by someone close to me . I take a breath in, soften my jaw, and bring my attention back to John. (I make a mental note that I need to talk about this transference with my supervisor). He removes his hat, folds it delicately and tucks it neatly into the top left pocket of his jacket. My eyes are drawn to his right ear. It is lacerated. He catches my eye and smiles.

'Aye, that was my younger days, a guy came after me wi' a machete… same wi' the fingers' and he waves them in front of his face. He does not appear to be boastful, he looks utterly exhausted. He does indeed look like he has had enough.

I nod.

Our session, I realise, is taking the form of a timeline of when he began his criminal career. He starts at the beginning. Nine years of age, drug running for the local gangs. Dodging school, cycling about the streets delivering packages. I remember his hesitance at signing the confidentiality agreement, he didn't spend time reading it, instead he asked 'where do I sign?' I have come to learn the signs of people who have difficulty reading. I asked him how good his reading was. I have learnt to overcome my own awkwardness in asking this because I've met so many men with similar pasts who have the reading age of young children. It makes managing therapy sessions a lot easier once that is understood.

His voice is surprisingly soft. He makes no eye contact with me as he speaks. He switches his gaze from the bottom right-hand side of the room to the top left. Describing his memories to me in vivid detail. Normally I would attend to this observation but instead I find myself leaning forward in my chair and holding my breath. I am transfixed. He talks me through the various 'positions' of responsibility and the sense of 'brotherhood' and 'family' it gave him. (I can relate to this; I witnessed this in my brother too). He is talking about his past historical criminal activities. I ask myself; "did he do time for these? Do I need to report these?" I remind him again of our confidentiality agreement. He nods. I listen on.

This has the feel of a confessional. The energy in the room has changed.

My first sense is of every fibre of my body going on high alert. This feels like it is crossing a boundary, crossing an invisible threshold into unchartered territory. I feel like an 'Etch-a-Sketch' where all the shards are standing rigidly to attention. I have heard many lived experience gang members tell their stories, but this has a different energy to it, this feels like he's going to tell me about something current. I am aware I am holding my breath, preparing for impact.

I realise I am in fight or flight mode. I feel as heavy as lead, unable to move my vocal cords or my arms. I muster up the strength. The tension feels like a lead cloak I need to shrug off my shoulders. I understand that I need to unquiet myself, activate myself and remind him of our confidentiality agreement. I hear my own quiet scratchy voice tell him again about the confidentiality agreement. I ask him again, my throat beating, pushing air through… "do you understand?" I ask, my voice raspy. My head at a slight angle, looking him straight in the eye, holding his gaze… a straight solid line trying to penetrate his conscious mind.

"If you tell me things that cause me concern about your behaviour or any harm you have caused and will cause, I will need to tell the police, do you get that?". He nods and carries on.

He continues…

In all honesty I am both spellbound and speechless. He continues, telling me about the crimes he has been involved in. I feel like I am in a slow-motion bubble with him. I check in with myself, 'did he hear me when I said that about the confidentiality?' What exactly is happening here?

And then he tells me…about that one last job. I notice my throat tightening further, a gentle hand grip slowly squeezing. I am leaning forward with my elbows on my knees. I am absolutely still. My armpits feel like ice and without moving my gaze or position I place my left hand surreptitiously under my right arm pit to feel the ice cubes that must be there. My mouth is desert dry and I can feel my heart beating through my shirt. But my mind, oh my mind… I hear the voice inside my head shout… 'this is amazing! I want to know more; how does he prepare himself before a job? Perhaps we could use that focus on managing his stutter. Suddenly I am aware that when working with non-criminals I use what is a strength for them to 'template' and draw from for their current issue. I tell myself I could do this here.

And it is here that I believe I crossed the line.

I remember the feeling of resignation. I remember thinking "OK if we are going there then I want to understand how you manage yourself before a job, what is happening for you, before, during and after?" I told myself "How often will I get this opportunity to ask these questions?"

It is here that I should have stopped him. I could have stood up to visually demonstrate my dis-ease with his lack of response to my verbal requests of confidentiality.

Instead, I leant in and listened, as I would with any client. I listened out for the techniques he uses to calm his mind. I wanted to understand what this man does to steady his mind before a job. I noticed that as he spoke about 'his work' he was without the stutter. He was a man transformed. He spoke about meditation and getting a sense of what he was feeling in his body before a job. That standing in front of his full-length mirror and practising his words and facial expressions was fundamental in him building a picture of how he had to see himself in order to do the job. Techniques well used by most people day to day.

As he told me this, he pushed his massive knuckles down on his knees and stood up and out of his chair, my neck craning upwards to follow his trajectory. Suddenly I felt very, very small. My mind was being blown, but my body was frozen still. Turning towards the wall, he quietly hissed profanities through a severed mouth. The bulk of his shoulders visible through his jacket as he pointed his partially fingerless digits towards the wall.

As he turned around, lowered his head to sit down, I swallowed and rolled my tongue around my mouth quickly.

It felt like an eternity as I sat there. I was so taken by my mind and body reaction. What the hell was going on for me that my mind was so keen, but my body clearly wasn't? How can my body be in shock but my mind not? A small, slightly husky voice gradually getting louder and stronger said...

"I have to remind you of our confidentiality agreement..."

And then afterwards...

I explained that I was concerned about the welfare of the person he was 'going to give a beating to.' He told me the tools he would use, how he would do it and what he would be saying as he did it. At no point did I get the sense he was boasting or trying to impress me. I did however get a sense that he was trying to justify why it had to be done.

Wishing to get some form of validation from me, he lifted his left hand up, displaying his large thumb upwards, looking me straight in the eye. As he slowly turned his thumb from upwards, rotating it to halfway, holding my gaze, continuing to rotate downwards, I nodded.

Our time was up, the session was over. Automatically I performed as I always do, by closing the session and arranging the next.

He hesitated, looked me directly in the eye, bowed his head and nodded, he understood there was to be no harm. However, I began to doubt if he would keep to the agreement, it felt very real, I feared he was planning to continue to do harm. Suddenly a fear for my own safety and that of my family began to grow inside of me. Suddenly I felt so vulnerable.

I felt sick... My mind racing... I was thinking...

"If I grass him up…what are the consequences for me and my family?"

"He could find me. He likes me now, but that doesn't mean very much."

I was also aware that I had another client waiting outside. "Ok after this next client," I told myself, "I need to contact his next of kin" His "healthy adult barrier" he had called her… "Everything has to go through her."

After seeing my final client of the day albeit in a reeling fog, I locked up and made a beeline for the phone. I spoke with John's partner and explained my concerns. I could hear her thinking; she thanked me for telling her and said she'd speak with him. She did not sound angry, she sounded disappointed…

"I told him to stop all that, we're alright for money you see" She was cordial and calm, her tone kind. I felt a sudden rush of goodwill swell up in my chest… remembering the softer parts of him that I had witnessed… "He's a good man" I said. I heard the crack of saliva as she smiled… "that I know."

I phoned my supervisor. He picked up immediately. As I told him about the circumstances, he observed that my voice sounded strangled. I had a residual thickening in my throat. I felt close to tears, finally free to speak…

"I think I need to phone the police; he gave a time, place and person" I was like a child hanging on to the phone with both hands waiting to be given the correct information, hoping he would tell me not to contact the police.

He told me not to. Relief.

My supervisor's voice was earnest and sure. I felt a wave of relief, my throat softening slightly, my shoulders relaxing. Tears of relief blurred my vision, my head was pounding. My body slackening.

"No, there will be no need for that. You've informed his partner and he said he would not be doing it."

I spoke at length, fragmented speak, disjointed, about the concerns for me and my family.

"What if he finds me, but what if…"

The last 'job' was to occur that weekend. My husband and I had planned a trip kayaking from Kinlochbervie to Cape Wrath, which we did. I can tell you this… I would rather suffer the threat of the high seas and gnarly winds than endure being on land looking over my shoulder, listening out for any noise. When we returned to land, I did indeed spend the next nine months looking over my shoulder. And it came to a point, the noise so loud, so continuous in my head, I felt utterly mentally shattered by my own hyper vigilance. I found myself saying out loud in a bold strong voice, my children's heads turning from the TV to the kitchen, their mouths open, eyes wide as I shouted into the half-made lasagne…

"I will not live in fear!"

I had one more session with my client after this experience. He informed me he had taken his son to the races instead. I could feel my body begin to thaw. It was going to be OK… for him? For me? I must have smiled because he looked at me, my hand on my heart, he smiled and nodded back. "God John, I'm so proud of you." The one last job he didn't do.

As I closed our last session together, he stood up and as I turned to place my notepad down on my seat, he was closer than I had expected. I was aware not to step back, I couldn't anyway because my chair was flush against the wall. He bent down and wove his arms under and through mine. Lifting me up like a doll, my arms up like a ballerina. I remember thinking I have two choices here: scream or embrace his embrace.

So, I hugged him back, lowering my arms, tentatively tapping the bulk of his muscle and then genuinely leaning into him, hugging his mass, my legs dangling off the ground. And he whispered…

"Thankyou."

Three key takeaways from this experience:

1. **Boundary setting and confidentiality:** The therapist's experience highlights the importance of setting and maintaining clear boundaries with clients, especially regarding confidentiality and the limits thereof. This case underscores the delicate balance between professional curiosity and ethical responsibility. Do not cross out of the boundary due to your own curiosity!

2. **Managing personal reactions and safety:** The therapist's intense personal and physical reactions to the client's disclosures illustrate the importance of recognising and managing ones own emotions and ensuring personal safety. The case emphasises the need to be aware of transference and countertransference dynamics and their impact on therapeutic practice.

3. **Supervision and support systems:** The pivotal role of supervision in navigating challenging cases is evident. Supervision provided critical guidance and emotional support, helping the therapist process the experience and make informed decisions about client management and personal safety.

How did this experience help you improve your practice?

This experience significantly enhanced my awareness of my own boundaries and the importance of maintaining them firmly and has changed my entire career trajectory. I was set on working in prisons. Having this first-hand experience has helped me be supremely focused on boundaries. The moment I feel a potential bump moving towards my boundary, I listen and act first time. It underscored the necessity of balancing curiosity with professional responsibility, teaching me to prioritise safety and ethical considerations even in moments of intense interest. I learnt to recognise the physical and emotional cues within myself that indicate when I am becoming too enmeshed in a client's narrative. This understanding helps me stay grounded and focused on the therapeutic goals rather than being swept up by the client's story.

How did clinical supervision support you through the experience? Did you access any additional supports?

Supervision was crucial in navigating this complex situation. My supervisor provided immediate compassion, guidance and reassurance, helping me process the intensity of the session and the potential risks involved. His advice not to contact the police, given the partner's involvement and reassurance, was instrumental in alleviating my anxiety and helping me focus on my role. Additionally, discussing the experience with my supervisor allowed me to vent my fears and concerns, which was cathartic and essential for my mental well-being. I did not access any other formal support but found significant relief in discussing my fears with my supervisor, which helped mitigate the heightened sense of vigilance and fear I experienced post-session. I read up on articles where therapists have had to contact the police and the impact it had on them. It was comforting to recognise similar experiences to mine.

What insights have you gained from being curious about the experience and from the process of self-reflection?

This experience highlighted the powerful impact of transference and the importance of beingaware of my own reactions and biases. It taught me that while curiosity is valuable in therapy, it must be tempered with a strong ethical framework and self-awareness. I realised the need for clear, repeated communication about confidentiality and the importance of ensuring the client fully understands it. Reflecting on this session made me acutely aware of the physical manifestations of my emotional state and the necessity of addressing them promptly. This self-reflection reinforced the importance of ongoing personal and professional development to manage complex and potentially dangerous situations effectively. I am very glad I had this experience; it has taught me so much. I learnt that I am resilient in the face of this fear - my mind was! I coped and I have adjusted my way of practice because of this. It also provided for me a real, human experience which helped me understand that I do not want to work in prisons. I do not want to have to look over my shoulder. I completed my BSc (Hons) in Forensic Psychology this year, having studied over five years. It was something I needed to do, to understand why it is that people cause harm. How attachment, childhoods and the emotional need to be part of something is so strong, even if it means becoming involved in gangs, I do get that.

What guidance and learning would you offer other professionals?

- **Maintain clear boundaries:** Always prioritise ethical boundaries and client safety over curiosity. Reinforce confidentiality agreements clearly and repeatedly.
- **Listen to your body:** Be aware of physical and emotional signals during sessions. These cues can indicate when you are becoming too involved or when a situation may be crossing professional boundaries.
- **Utilise supervision:** Regular supervision is vital. It provides an essential space for debriefing, gaining perspective, and receiving support during challenging situations.
- **Prepare for intensity:** Be prepared for intense sessions by having a clear plan for debriefing and self-care afterward. Recognise the impact such sessions can have on your mental health and take steps to mitigate this.
- **Continual learning:** Engage in continuous self-reflection and professional development to enhance your ability to manage complex cases. This includes understanding your own triggers and learning effective techniques to handle them.
- **Client understanding:** Ensure clients fully understand the Confidentiality agreement and its limitations. This may require multiple explanations and checks for understanding throughout the therapeutic process.

Chapter Ten

The Pessimists Within: When Unresolved Inner Conflict Impacts the Counselling Relationship

Alison Carter

The Journey

This is my journey
My journey through life
Where taking trips is common place
Where it's plain to see the price
With forewarning of the duration
And more than that the destination
But a journey my friend
Is a road with no end
It's a road I'll be travelling on and on
Now if I were to journey beside you
Helping you make your own way
What will you find there
With me close behind, say
Would that be the wakening of a new day?
How can I walk when you're walking
And know how to run when you run?
If I had a notion of your deepest emotion
And look at the world from a place within you
Oh, what will I do when your journey
Arouses my innermost fear?
Would I have the strength then
To stay till the end when
My own heart is hurting
My way is not clear

I hope that our travelling together
Through routes of the roughest terrain
When a new day is dawning
The heat of the morning
Shall help us to keep to the path we are on

This is my journey
My journey through life
Where taking trips is common place
Where it's plain to see the price
With forewarning of the duration
And more than that the destination
But a journey my friend
Is a road with no end
It's a road I'll be travelling on and on

I wrote the lyrics to this song in 1998, towards the end of my diploma in counselling at Strathclyde University as I was learning what it meant to metaphorically walk beside myclients in their journey of discovery whilst exploring my own inner world. Over the years, my clients' journeys, as it says in the song, 'arouse my innermost fear,' (or other strong emotions). At times like these in an ideal world, I would immediately think, "I know what this is about." But of course, it's rarely that simple. Certainly, in the early days of counselling I would regularly encounter reactions in myself I simply could not understand. Even today, albeit less frequently as I know myself better, something unexpected will enter my life, once again arousing my curiosity and sending me on yet another journey of self-discovery.

Background

Having worked as a person-centred therapist for over 20 years across NHS, EAP and private practice, I also work as a well-being consultant, and trainer and have held various senior clinical roles in several organisations.

My working life began in nursing and in particular, paediatric nursing. It was through this occupation that I first became interested in counselling. My motive was one of feeling inadequate when it came to providing emotional support to the parents of seriously ill and dying children. I can pinpoint the turning point to one evening on night shift, actively avoiding being the receiving nurse to parents who had lost their baby to cot death earlier that day. I clearly remember thinking, "I need to do something about this." I quickly sourced a two-day introduction to counselling course through the hospital where I worked. On day one of that course as we practiced in counselling skills triads, I remember thinking, 'this is what I want to do'. Not for a minute had I anticipated, by trying to improve my communication skills, I would take a different career path. I quickly enrolled on an introduction to counselling course through a local further education college then progressed to the certificate in counselling skills at Strathclyde University, going on to complete my diploma in counselling in 1998. At the age of 38 I became a fully employed counsellor working in the NHS and EAP. My career took off at a rate of knots, moving quickly through the ranks from telephone counsellor to clinical manager during the following 20 years. Throughout my counselling career, I have maintained a private practice, studied CBT and trauma response, and became a c linical and w ell-being s upervisor. Currently, I maintain my private practice as I work towards the latter part of my working life.

The client

One client who aroused strong emotions was in the early years of working as a counsellor. Tanya came to see me at my private practice. When asked if I ever 'got it wrong,' this is the client (not her real name) who springs to mind. In this chapter I have explored the experience anew from my current perspective, with several more years' experience under my belt.

Tanya attended counselling for about 14 months, mainly on a weekly basis. Her reason for seeking counselling were her feelings around her ex-partner whom she described as having left her to be with another woman.

From the start it was evident she did not trust easily, and through offering the core conditions of acceptance and empathy, we were able to establish, as far as I could ascertain, a fairly mutual and trusting relationship. In this description, I deliberately omitted to include the third core condition of congruence, as here lay my challenge. I noticed that as therapy progressed, I found it increasingly difficult to fully accept my client as she expressed her anger, frustration and, in my view, negativity towards her life and almost everyone in it. I was aware my own frustration was getting in the way of full acceptance and struggled with how to remain authentic in the counselling relationship, and to find a way of being congruent.

Tanya was the daughter of highly academic, intellectual parents. Her father, she described as a critical and relentless fault finder both professionally and in his parenting style. She admitted to being highly sensitive to criticism connected to her experience with her father.

Tanya described working in a job which was well below her own professional capabilities and qualifications. She suspected this was related to her fear of getting it wrong, so keeping in safe territory where this was less likely to happen. Tanya, despite being in her 40s would describe life as, "filling time up until you die." She described feeling like a victim (my words), in her personal situation and in her working life.

She was very positive towards her children except when it came to their relationship with their father, her ex-partner which she felt had a detrimental impact on her relationship with them.

Whilst I was sure I did not dislike my client, it became increasingly difficult to manage my own reaction of impatience, frustration and I began to dread our sessions together.

After a great deal of discussion and exploration in supervision, I decided to share some of my observations and what I perceived as her being 'stuck in her negative views'. Tanya did not respond well to this feedback and came to the following session telling me she had elicited the view of friends and family who all disagreed. She told me she had no doubt that I 'meant well' but she was hugely disappointed. She ended therapy soon after. Despite this difficult ending, she would text me from time to time and wish me well.

The counsellor

To help give context to my process in this situation, I shall tell my story.

Being the youngest child of two very different parents presented me with challenges as I inherited very opposing traits from both. Namely the optimist, my father, and the pessimist, my mother.

My father I would describe as a volatile and extreme extrovert, an active expressor of raw and untamed emotions both positive, (the highly creative party animal), and negative, (with covert and overt fury and angry outbursts). Alongside him was my mother. Highly anxious, introverted and with a low self-esteem she projected onto her family. She was also an attentive and loving individual interspersed with volatile and unpredictable bouts of self- sabotaging behaviour as witnessed by my two siblings and me. She lived her life in fear of the judgement of others and this too was projected onto the family. She regularly acted from a passive-aggressive stance, making life somewhat unpredictable. The conflict these opposing traits which my parents possessed was evident in their everyday interaction, regularly resulting in angry outbursts from both, primarily to each other but invariably impacting upon my own and my siblings' behaviours. We each learnt and inherited a concoction of traits in our own unique ways serving to add to the already complex family dynamics. Thankfully, despite their differences, they shared a real sense of adventure, affording our family a life of variety, exploration, excitement and very rarely boredom. Life was an unpredictable adventure.

Throughout my life, and in particular from my 30's onwards, I began to piece together the impact my family dynamics had on how I live my life. I was aware of the inner struggle I experienced between my optimistic extrovert I valued so much and the pessimistic introvert which I fought against as I struggled to moderate the former. At the time of my work with Tanya, I was some way along the voyage of discovery but unfortunately for both client and therapist, there was still work to be done.

Three key takeaways from this experience:
1. **Importance of self-awareness:** This experience highlighted the critical need for self-awareness in therapy. Recognising my own emotional reactions and biases allowed me to understand how they impacted my ability to provide unconditional positive regard and empathy to Tanya.
2. **Navigating client-therapist dynamics:** The challenges with Tanya underscored the importance of managing the dynamics between client and therapist. It became clear that finding a balance between authenticity and empathy is essential, especially when dealing with clients who evoke strong emotions
3. **Value of supervision:** The role of supervision was crucial in processing this challenging experience. It provided a space for reflection, support, and professional growth, emphasising the importance of seeking guidance and feedback from supervisors.

How did this experience help you improve your practice?
This experience has significantly improved my practice by making me more aware of my own emotional triggers and how they can affect the therapeutic relationship. It has taught me the importance of maintaining a high level of self-awareness and actively managing my responses to clients. I have also learnt to be more intentional in providing unconditional positive regard and empathy, even when it is challenging. Additionally, it has reinforced the value of honest and timely communication with clients about the dynamics of our interactions.

How did clinical supervision support you through the experience? Did you access any additional supports?

Supervision was instrumental in helping me navigate this difficult situation. My supervisor provided a safe space to explore my feelings of frustration and impatience, offering valuable insights and strategies for managing these emotions. This support helped me better understand my reactions and find ways to remain authentic and empathetic with Tanya. Beyond supervision, I also sought peer support and engaged in professional development opportunities focused on managing challenging client relationships and maintaining therapeutic boundaries.

What insights have you gained from being curious about the experience and from the process of self-reflection?

Through curiosity and self-reflection, I gained several key insights. I realised my reactions to Tanya were deeply influenced by my own unresolved issues and family dynamics. This understanding allowed me to approach my personal growth with greater compassion and curiosity. I also recognised the importance of ongoing self- reflection in therapy, as it helps to uncover unconscious biases and improve the therapeutic process. This experience reinforced the idea that therapy is a journey of mutual discovery, where both client and therapist can continuously learn and grow if each are looking inwards to their own unconscious process.

What guidance and learning would you offer other professionals?

- **Prioritise aelf-awareness:** Regularly engage in self-reflection to understand your own emotional triggers and biases. This awareness is crucial for providing effective and empathetic therapy. If necessary, engage in personal therapy.
- **Value supervision:** Make use of supervision to gain insights, support, and strategies for managing challenging client

interactions. It is an invaluable resource for professional growth.

- **Maintain boundaries and authenticity:** Strive to balance empathy with authenticity. Being honest with clients about the dynamics of your interactions can enhance trust and effectiveness in therapy.
- **Engage in continuous learning:** Attend workshops, seek peer support, and pursue professional development opportunities to stay informed and improve your practice.
- **Reflect on client interactions:** Regularly reflect on your sessions and clientinteractions to identify areas for improvement and gain deeper insights into the therapeutic process. This ongoing reflection helps in maintaining a high standard of care.

Additional thoughts

Negativity is a feeling or view expressed by many clients from time to time. What was it about Tanya in particular that I found so difficult? I don't have a definitive answer to this question, even now. I have, however, reflected on my own process of self-awareness. At the time when I worked with Tanya, whilst being aware of my own inner conflict and also its origin, I had yet to reach a level of self-acceptance. I didn't appreciate that the adventurer in me ("a road with no end.....a road I'll be travelling on and on"), was at odds with Tanya's resigned, "filling up time till you die" mantra. This prevented me from fully owning my own unresolved inner conflict and hence I projected this onto my client. With most clients I worked with, I would generally see some movement in relation to their feelings of negativity and pessimism. For those who were not ready to make the changes necessary to move forward, I can only assume they would have finished counselling in one way or another, planned or unplanned. Tanya on the other hand, despite feeling stuck and unable to move forward, continued to persevere with counselling and, I regret, had more staying power than I. I believe that I failed Tanya as I simply could not resolve my own inner conflict at the time. You could say I was also stuck in my own process, mirroring what I was experiencing with Tanya.

Chapter Eleven

When All That Could Go Wrong Goes Wrong: Managing Risk in Remote Private Practice.

Dr Maria Georgiou Shippi

The recent global COVID-19 pandemic was the catalyst for tele-psychology to be popularised (Pierce et al., 2021), researched and given permanent status as a method of offering psychological services.

Both practitioners and clients had concerns regarding connecting online. For example, how might technology impact the therapeutic alliance? Can the emotional dimensions of the therapeutic relationship be honoured online? It appears that it can (Stiles-Shields, et al., 2021) and remote therapy is effective for a range of age groups and conditions (Hilty, et al., 2013; Varker et al., 2019; Turgoose et al., 2018).

Professional bodies like the American Psychological Association [APA] and the British Psychological Society [BPS], have created guidelines for working with clients online (APA, 2013, 2020; BPS, 2020). These guidelines paint a picture of what one must keep in mind when working online and the practicalities of doing so which essentially transfer one's practice online.

The guidelines specify that the general proficiency and ethical standards apply in tele-psychology, and the APA (2013) makes recommendations regarding the handling of risk in remote practice. Specifically, practitioners need to:

> *"make reasonable effort to identify and learn how to access relevant and appropriate emergency resources in the client's/patient's local area, [...], prepare a plan to address any lack of appropriate resources, [...] make reasonable effort to discuss with and provide all clients/patients with clear written instructions as to what to do in an emergency."*

In my case, I am an accredited in two countries, the UK and Cyprus. I take on clients from both countries and maintain two professional bases. Clients at times move to different countries and thus, I have found myself working with clients across the UK, Europe and the Middle East. I had to enhance my literacy and regarding how different countries manage risk, legislation, and context of care, repeatedly. The learning curve has alway felt intense.

In establishing and running my own private practice, I have developed my own intake process and assessment objectives. It involves a detailed exploration of the risk attached to each case, by enquiring about any active or past suicidal ideation, suicide attempts and self-harm. From experience in working with clients with active suicidal intent and past training in suicide prevention, I am aware that clients with active suicide risk might require more support in-between sessions, primarily because of their high levels of distress. Generally, my clients have not had active suicidal risk at onboarding. This helped to create a sense of dependability on my intake and safety processes, until those were not enough.

The first step of the intake process is initiated prior to the initial appointment. After a client makes contact and we reach an agreement that we will explore the potential of our therapeutic co-operation, I forward the therapeutic contract to the client over email and request that it is completed and returned to me prior to our scheduled appointment.

Prior to what constituted a major learning curve, I requested client's contact details, home address, GP details, and one emergency contact. This was requested to make sure I had enough information to ensure the client's safety from the first point of contact. My therapeutic contract also covers how confidentiality is maintained and the exclusions to this.

The therapeutic contract is conceptualised as an active organism, being very much alive and changing based on needs, perceptions, and experience. In some ways it is and can be co-created with clients and it functions as my 'professional security blanket.' It enables a sense of comfort by knowing that pathways of and for action have been paved, are well organised and streamlined. By having these pathways set out, I will not need to travel down "The Road Less Travelled" (Peck, 1978). I will travel down a path that I have prepared for and know of, in a moment of high stress and urgency. For many years my therapeutic contract was exactly that. I could refer clients back for clarity, I could amend it to make it fit to specific clients' needs.

All was fine, until a series of unfortunate events unfolded. Right there and then, the established pathways fell short and I needed to replan, act, and negotiate while in a state of heightened anxiety, stress, sleepiness and panic. It was 11pm my time, and 9pm for my client. I had gotten ready to go to bed. I conducted my usual inspection of electronics' battery life, with eyes half closed from the tiredness of the day. My work phone was low on battery, and I plugged it in to charge. I noticed a text message from a client, from now on referred to as Bob (details included and relating to Bob have been changed to preserve his confidentiality). The preview bubble of his text read "Goodbye…". I opened the message, while taking deep breaths to regulate my anxiety. I tried hard to put my thoughts in order to initiate the safety protocol:

1. Contact the client and assess the immediacy of risk, if necessary.
2. Access my e-files for the emergency contact details, due to this being after the normal GP working hours.
3. If necessary, inform Bob I will be contacting their emergency contact and do so.
4. Contact my clinical supervisor for support and validation of the action plan.

Despite knowing what to do and how to do it, I felt extremely distressed as the possibility of making a mistake could prove costly to Bob's life. This was the first time I handled a suicide attempt in private practice. I felt fear as I was holding all clinical responsibility for Bob's safety. I contacted Bob and was left confused by our conversation. Bob was not forthcoming with information but disclosed taking a higher dose of his prescribed medication. This was not Bob's usual mode of relaying his thoughts or events. I reflected my confusion to Bob and shared that since I had no way to assess the level of risk to his safety, I would contact his emergency contact, from now on referred to as Jack.

Bob exhibited high levels of distress when he realised that his privacy was about to be compromised. He started crying, hyperventilating, and insisted that he preferred contacting Jack himself. Respecting Bob's agency, I agreed to wait for five minutes while he contacted Jack. We made an agreement regarding safekeeping, which included that Bob would request Jack to join him in his home. The aim of this was for Jack to seek help if Bob was to experience any side effects from the substances he had consumed. Moreover, we agreed that Bob would debrief me on the process i.e., contact was made, Jack is on his way, Jack arrived etc.

During those 5 minutes, I contacted my supervisor sharing the steps I decided to take. I decided to allow Bob to act on his own behalf because of his exhibited cognitive and emotional functionality. Pairing this with having no way of assessing the immediacy of risk, created a need to act tentatively since I was aware of Bob's sensitivity to a diminished sense of personal agency. I specified that I would do so while maintaining a close watch for clues of Bob's cognitive deterioration, which could infer serious side effects resulting from his consumption of medication.

The five minutes had passed, and Bob had not made contact to debrief me on his process. To make matters worse he was not responding to my calls. Instead, he texted his disagreement regarding the agreed safety plan and announced his unwillingness to engage with it. In my mind, the level of risk to Bob's safety was now far greater since his trustworthiness was compromised. I could no longer rely on his estimations of ability to maintain his safety nor his reports of feeling ok. Bob's evasiveness was perceived as having a function. It was aimed to prolong his privacy by delaying safety related procedures. From that point on, the best practice approach would be to act as if this was a high-risk situation.

I felt that my emotions were gathering momentum, and I was fearful of how that might impact my professional decision making. It was obvious that I could not rely on Bob's promises to act on his own behalf. I felt extremely uncomfortable knowing I needed to act against his wishes, despite knowing it was necessary. I also felt resentful since I was forced to act for his own benefit while tilting the established power balance. A balance I had worked hard to build and honour. I felt that I was undoing all my good work. My supervisor, with whom I was in contact throughout this time, normalised my emotional reactivity regarding breaking confidentiality, and we discussed the actions I would take with regards to Bob. These were broken down as follows:

1. Keeping Bob informed of the steps I would take and the rationale attached to my decision.
2. Contact Jack.
3. Request that Jack visits Bob;
   a. Request a debrief from Jack following his arrival at Bob's home; and
   b. A description of Bob's current state i.e. lucid, cognitively aware, able to communicate etc.
4. If necessary, contact the emergency services.

Following informing Bob of the above, I was happy to observe that Bob was lucid and able to repeatedly express his feelings towards my decision making. I took this to infer that the level of risk was not extremely high, but since I was not able to place it on any other part of the continuum, actions would be taken, nonetheless.

To my disbelief, when I contacted Jack, my call went directly to voicemail. I left a voice message, texted, and emailed explicitly stating my name, my profession, relationship to Bob, reason for contacting them (Jack was stated as the emergency contact) and the need to call me back. I contacted my supervisor yet again and informed her of the situation. Sharing my disbelief regarding Jack being unreachable, made it easier to hold my uncertainty and fear. My supervisor pointed out that even if Jack was not responding I still had the option of calling the emergency services. I allowed for a few minutes to pass, which felt like an eternity, but Jack had still not made contact. In the meantime, Bob kept texting, so I knew he was alive and coherent enough to express himself. I decided to call the emergency services, as I felt that time was of the essence.

I could not get through the stated extension number for the emergency services, servicing Bob's geographical location and calling 112/119 connected me with my own country's emergency services. My panic soared and my mind fluctuated in disbelief and desperation. I called my supervisor yet again and relayed the problem. Although we had not contracted for this, she agreed that she would call the emergency services on my behalf and relay Bob's information. Since she was living in the same country as Bob, calling 112 was an option.

While on that call, Jack called me back. I asked my supervisor to refrain from acting, and I took the call. I debriefed Jack on the need to visit Bob's home, and thankfully he was a few minutes away. I kept receiving texts from Bob and I let him know that Jack was on his way. Bob clearly expressed being displeased with having his privacy disturbed, his worries of how this would impact his relationship with Jack.

Throughout this, I felt empathy for Bob's expressed distress, and felt uneasy for challenging the way he showcased himself in the specific relationship. I could hear and sense his pain of being exposed, his vulnerabilities put on a show for others to see. Throughout my work with Bob, I had clearly seen, felt, related to, and perceived his need to control his life. To rely solely on himself to survive, his pain when important life decisions and matters of personal agency were overrun by others. I felt that I was leaving Bob behind by acting against his wishes. I felt terrible since my function in Bob's life had suddenly changed. From a person of trust and support I turned myself into a perpetrator of his past trauma, depriving him of his personal freedoms, options and dictating what would be next for him. I became all of this overnight, without my consent, and without his consent. I felt immense pain and anger. Anger towards Bob for forcing me to show up in a mode I am uncomfortable with and against how I am and want to be experienced as a practitioner.

In those moments, if I am being honest, I was doing just that. I was informing Jack of Bob's inner world, giving him partial insight towards the fact that there was a risk to Bob's safety, insight that if it was up to Bob, Jack would never have known. While feeling all of this and waiting for an update, Jack called to say that Bob was not letting him in, but he was assuring him that he was fine. Jack wanted to believe him. So did I. However, I relayed to Jack that the best way of ensuring Bob's safety was for Bob to be examined by the emergency services, since I had no information nor the capacity to assess the impact of the substances Bob had consumed.

My conversation with Jack was multifaceted. Firstly, and in relation to Bob, it functioned as a negotiation aiming to persuade Jack to call the emergency services, since I was unable to do so. Secondly, in relation to Jack, it involved supporting him through the pain and uncertainty of how his actions would impact his relationship with Bob. Thirdly, and in relation to myself, it involved a lot of self-control to hold both objectives in mind simultaneously. Jack agreed to call the emergency services, and I asked to be informed of their conclusions. Following their examination of Bob, they stated that although Bob had consumed something (what was not disclosed even to them, and they found no evidence), it did not pose any threats to his physical health.

I took what felt to be the deepest breath I took the whole night. I debriefed my supervisor that the matter was successfully handled and booked myself a supervision session to explicitly discuss what had happened and potential therapeutic paths forward. Bob and I had plans to connect online a few days later, and I felt like I could use the time to reflect.

Support through supervision

The support I received through supervision related to both the handling of the event as it unfolded, learning, and implementing the new insights to my practice.

With regards to the handling of the event, my supervisor played a vital role in how I handled the multiple reconsiderations of action.

She helped me handle my emotional reactivity and stress when all that could go wrong went wrong. Her flexibility in meeting my needs as a supervisee was essential. If Jack had remained unreachable and I had no way of contacting the emergency services, I would be legally and ethically liable for failing to meet the most basic element of working with clients; the requirement of acting to ensure clients' safety.

In terms of my learning, I was able to freely explore and reflect on my emotions, without holding back, because of the accepting and non-judgemental nature of our relationship. I focused on feeling disoriented and hopeless by realising that although I had tried my best to handle the crisis, obstacles kept appearing. I expressed feeling petrified from realising that if Bob's actions were more harmful, he could have died in the time it took to jump through all the unexpected hurdles. I mentioned that I doubted my ability to work remotely and my capacity to help people from a distance. I expressed my unwillingness to rely on chance and probabilities in handling an element of risk ever again. Through supervision I was helped to decipher the way forward. By being able to be fully open and vulnerable in supervision, we focused on things that could be put in place to streamline my safety protocol.

In thinking of how I would handle things differently if I was in the same country as Bob, it was evident that I would be able to act without wasting any time. Convincing the emergency contact that action was indeed necessary and supporting them through their fear of creating a rupture to their relationship should not be a mediating factor that enables me to meet my ethical and professional responsibilities towards Bob. My supervisor pointed out that although this was far simpler and optimised, it was not an option. Given the newfound learning of being unable to call 112/119, if I was to continue working remotely, then I would need to solve the problem of accessing the emergency services. Thought went into what that would look like. If eliminating these elements was not an option, then minimising their potential for interference was the next best thing. This is what I decided on:

- I would need two emergency contacts, in case the first is not available.
- Emergency contacts need to reside in the same country as the client, so they are able to access the emergency services if need be.
- The emergency contact needs to have high willingness and readiness for action.
- Action from the emergency contact will be required in the case that: an event takes place out of a GP's normal working hours; and if the stated extension number to access the emergency services is unavailable.
- Being respectful and appreciative that creating a rupture to a valued relationship is painful, I could offer my support to emergency contacts after the chaos is dealt with.

Three key takeaways from this experience:

1. The above elements are non-negotiable components of my contract. Additionally, the contracting phase involves both clients and their emergency contacts. I have created an appendix which clients forward to their chosen emergency contacts. It involves providing me with their details and their consent to contact the appropriate service in the case of an emergency. If they agree, they sign the document and forward it back to me.

2. To deal with potential reactivity and/or concerns from both parties, I allocate time to clarify and explain to all involved why this is important and necessary. To ensure these elements are discussed without any time pressures, initial appointments are not booked immediately. Initial appointments are booked the week following the initial contact. It is also explicitly stated that if the contract and the appendix are not completed prior to our initial appointment, the appointment will be rescheduled.

3. As I expected, some clients have chosen to not co-operate with me because of my new contracting and intake process.

That is a cost that I am willing to bear. I now view this as a filtering process. The resulting client pool and their supporting networks provide a certainty that we will co-operate to manage a threat to someone's safety. The worst-case scenario of managing risk remotely, is that I might need to rely on other people to contact a service. I prefer knowing that in such cases, people are willing and ready to act.

What insights have you gained from being curious about the experience and from the process of self-reflection?

This is not an element that sat well with me nor was the fact that I felt I was sharing a component of my professional responsibility with emergency contacts. Through supervision-aided reflection, I realised that I perceived the cooperation between myself and the emergency contacts as forcing people to hold to a level of uncertainty they are not trained to handle. Despite this being uncomfortable, it was assimilated in my new reality for remote practice. The experience with Bob functioned as an awakening. Time efficiency in risk management needs to be protected, enabled, and taken as seriously as safety. I tried to allow my discomfort to practically shape my safekeeping protocol. Thought went into how I would communicate with emergency contacts, what information I would relay to them so they can appropriately relay information to the emergency services, without feeling unnecessarily burdened.

During the twists and turns of acting to explore the threats and ensure Bob's safety, I needed to withstand the force and momentum of various emotions. I was unsure of whether my relationship with Bob could recover from breaking confidentiality, despite knowing that all the steps I took that evening were necessary. My mindset was very much focused on minimising the potential rupture to my relationship with Bob. I hoped he would forgive me for acting against his wishes, for taking control while knowing he spent many years feeling helpless, for taking down the mask he was wearing in his relationship. A mask he worked hard to create, a mask he relied on to keep himself safe. Having all these feelings allowed me to take a firm stance in activating the safety protocol, and maintain a respectful attitude towards Bob's sensitivities and preferences. This empathetic attitude was showcased throughout my communication with Bob by sharing the rationale which informed my decision making and actions. This helped showcase a co-operative element in the moment-to-moment action and recalibration of the safety protocol. Additionally, I was able to empathically relate to his voiced concerns, normalise and challenge parts of his fears and help him cope by reminding him of skills and strengths we had built in therapy. For example, when he was fearful of how this would impact his relationship with Jack, we discussed occasions of being vulnerable and how that served to strengthen their bond. My experience with Bob showcased that a strong therapeutic alliance and insight of clients' sensitivities, strengths and ways of communicating was essential for informing my professional judgements. Having such insights, allowed for flexibility and individualisation in the process of keeping Bob safe and minimised the rupture of the therapeutic alliance. We continued working together, exploring what led to him risking his safety, created his own personal safety plan, and parted ways amicably and respectfully for other reasons.

I firmly believe that not having such therapeutic insight would prove detrimental in a similar scenario. Professionally, my ability to reach conclusions and balance being firm with holding the space for clients, would be compromised in the presence of an unstable therapeutic alliance. Thus, I decided I will not be initiating co-operations with clients with an active suicide intent. In the cases that clients develop a risk for suicide, then I will work through this with them, relying on our therapeutic alliance to inform my judgments.

What guidance and learning would you offer other professionals?

Based on my experience, I offer the following guidance to other professionals:

- **Establish robust safety protocols:** Ensure you have a comprehensive and flexible risk management plan. Include multiple emergency contacts and detailed procedures for various crisis scenarios.
- **Seek and utilise supervision:** Develop a strong supervisory relationship and seek support during crises. Supervision can provide emotional and practical assistance, helping you navigate challenging situations effectively.
- **Maintain a strong therapeutic alliance:** Invest in building and maintaining a strong therapeutic relationship with clients. Understand their sensitivities, communication styles, and needs to inform your crisis management strategies.
- **Commit to continuous learning:** Embrace continuous professional development and reflective practice. Stay curious and open to learning from each experience to enhance your skills and preparedness for future challenges.

Final reflections and key take-aways

The above experience highlights the importance of a supportive supervisory alliance, where a practitioner is able to be open and honest regarding their emotions and professional needs. Emotions serve the function of signposts and can inform our judgement of professional competencies and decision making. In having experiences of negative supervision and researching the topic for my doctoral thesis (Shippi, 2017), I knew that such openness is required for learning and growing professionally. Thus, for me it is a professional requirement to have a supervisor that can offer me that, alongside guidance and intervention ideas that relate to therapeutic planning.

Private practice has many freedoms, and this was my experience of the dark side of freedom regarding remote practice. Taking a stance and publicly announcing that this is my limitation, this is what I need to practise safely and responsibly feels vulnerable. I choose to feel the discomfort of vulnerability than to risk being helpless. By being vulnerable I have gained confidence and trust in my ability to handle the worst-case scenario.

References

Abrams, Z. (2020). *How well is telepsychology working?* https://www. apa.org. https://www.apa.org/monitor/2020/07/cover-telepsychology

American Psychological Association (2023) COVID-19. (n.d.). https://www.apa.org. https://www.apa.org/topics/covid-19

American Psychological Association (2013).*Guidelines for the practice of telepsychology.* https://www.apa.org. https://www.apa.org/practice/ guidelines/telepsychology

British Psychological Society (2020). *Considerations for psychologists working with children and young people using online video platforms | BPS. (n.d.).* BPS. https://www.bps.org.uk/guideline/considerations-psychologists-working-children-and-young-people-using-online-video

Hilty, D. M., Ferrer, D. C., Parish, M. B., Johnston, B., Callahan, E. J., & Yellowlees, P. M. (2013). *The effectiveness of telemental health: a 2013 review. Telemedicine journal and e-health: the official journal of the American Telemedicine Association,* 19(6), 444–454. https://doi. org/10.1089/tmj.2013.0075

Pierce, B. S., Perrin, P. B., Tyler, C. M., McKee, G. B., & Watson, J. D. (2021). *The COVID-19 telepsychology revolution: A national study of pandemic-based changes in U.S. mental health care delivery. The American psychologist,* 76(1), 14–25. https://doi.org/10.1037/amp0000722

Shippi, G, M. (2017). *Unresolved negative experiences in supervision and growth: An exploration of the mediating factors promoting growth in counselling psychology trainees* [unpublished PsychD thesis]. Glasgow Caledonian University.

Stiles-Shields, C., Kwasny, M. J., Cai, X., & Mohr, D. C. (2014). *Therapeutic alliance in face-to-face and telephone-administered cognitive behavioral therapy. Journal of Consulting and Clinical Psychology,* 82(2), 349–354. https://doi.org/10.1037/a0035554

Turgoose, D., Ashwick, R., & Murphy, D. (2018). *Systematic review of lessons learnt from delivering tele-therapy to veterans with post-traumatic stress disorder. Journal of telemedicine and telecare,* 24(9), 575–585. https://doi.org/10.1177/1357633X17730443

Varker, T., Brand, R. M., Ward, J., Terhaag, S., & Phelps, A. (2019). *Efficacy of synchronous telepsychology interventions for people with anxiety, depression, posttraumatic stress disorder, and adjustment disorder: A rapid evidence assessment.* Psychological services, 16(4), 621–635. https://doi.org/10.1037/ser0000239

CHAPTER TWELVE

When Empathy Hurts: Bringing in a Neurobiological, Trauma Informed Perspective

Lizzy Pittock

The following chapter was written by Lizzy Pittock. Lizzy is a Glasgow-based, neurodivergent, queer, chronically ill, non-binary therapist who is a HCPC registered art psychotherapist which is a protected title. At the time of writing this chapter, Lizzy has over six years' post qualifying experience working with children, young people, and adults, now specialising in working with complex trauma. Lizzy is trained in EMDR and studying to be a clinical trauma professional. Lizzy works in both private practice and for a Scottish charity supporting victims of childhood sexual abuse.

For the purpose of this chapter and to protect the client's confidentiality, the examples Lizzy uses are a combination of experiences with different clients collected to form imaginary client examples.

When empathy hurts.

"Great, you made me feel like such an idiot! Thanks a lot Lizzy!" my client exclaimed followed by a long list of expletives. This moment followed an exploration of the client's safety seeking behaviours which they had noticed others in their life, including previous therapists, reacted to with fear. This client felt curious why I responded differently and calmly to these behaviours, so we had explored my perspective. With that, this client suddenly felt seen which was the very thing their defences were designed to protect them from. My understanding caused the client to feel unsafe and so their defences activated to attack by blaming and swearing at me.

Whenever this happens in the therapy room, I think back to one of the first clients I worked with who expressed their discomfort by attacking me. The client was a young person who I worked with in my early career. This young person was described by the adults in their life as misbehaving, stubborn, and nasty-tempered amongst other negative labels and there was a sense for me of everyone having given up on them. Getting to know them, I could see the client did not respond well to any form of connection and reacted in violent ways.

For the first few sessions the client pushed every boundary possible, attempting to trash the room and reject any attempt I made at connecting with them. The therapeutic boundaries seemed challenging for them to accept and they consistently tried to intimidate me into complying with their wishes. To say it was a fraught beginning would be an understatement. A few sessions in, realising their attempts to make me abandon the boundaries were not working, the client began creating art and describing stories about how they would murder and eat me. The client used such graphic descriptions, I would often feel physically sick listening to them. They studied me closely in these interactions, barely looking at their page but instead were intensely focused on my face. They responded to my bids for connections and attempts at understanding with a sinister smile. They had such a glint in their eye of such enjoyment that I felt disturbed.

Throughout the entire time I worked with this client, I took them to each of my management and clinical supervision sessions. With their gaze being on me, I knew my reaction was what they were looking for but I felt so confused why they wanted to attack me like this. I recognised this was likely the client communicating how they expected to be treated by others and their internal feelings but I felt flummoxed. Before working with this client, I felt I had a good understanding of why and how clients push the therapeutic boundaries. I had experienced clients trying to attack the space by trying to break things in the therapy room; clients who refused to leave at the end of the session; clients who hid away or had their back turned to me during the session; clients who talked over me and did not allow me any space; clients who tried to physically intimidate me; clients who rejected everything I said; clients who shut down; and so on. I had not yet come across or learnt of clients who specifically targeted the therapist with violence in this way.

I tried to explore what was happening with the client in different ways but nothing seemed to change. Each of these early sessions were the same. Nothing I seemed to do changed things. I had tried exploring if therapy was helpful with the client and by all accounts in their eyes and from the perspective of adults connected to them, it was. It seemed it was just me that felt uncomfortable.

Adding to my discomfort were the labels attributed to the client by my superiors of the time. In trying to understand the client's behaviour, the client was labelled as possibly experiencing serious mental health difficulties such as psychotic episodes. These labels made me feel so out of my depth as I was not confident I had the adequate experience to support such clients.

One day, about a third of the way through the time we worked together, the therapy sessions hit a turning point. The client had had to miss out on working on an art project in order to attend their therapy session. I had noticed how sad the client seemed on the way into the therapy room and offered them the option of doing something similar in the session. Their face lit up at this suggestion and they enjoyed creating some art alongside me. Towards the end of the session, the client's extremities were covered in paint. There was no sink in the room, so I provided a basin with warm water and a towel to clean up. Resting their hands in the water, the client's guard suddenly dropped. They told me about memories of being little and their bath time. Memories that suddenly came flooding in about the only caring adult they had had in their life who they had since lost contact with. They told me all about how painful it was to lose that person from their life and how their angry part scares people away to stop that from happening again. The client completely changed from this point. There were no more attacks on me and instead all their therapy work became focused on processing this loss.

I started looking more into the topic of trauma and realised my knowledge was lacking. In my training, the focus was on psychodynamic principles with very little on understanding or how to work with trauma. I got stuck into learning more about trauma-informed practice and learning about the nervous system, the window of tolerance, stress response, the brain, the impacts of trauma, the six stress responses, the different types of memory, dissociation, shame, and so on. This learning really helped in my understanding but also, in sharing this learning with my clients, helped my clients understand what was happening to them, reducing the shame and fear for all parties.

If we examine what happened with the client using the psychodynamic and attachment principles I was taught, this client had lost their only model of secure attachment and so unconsciously protected themself against this happening again. They felt terrified to let someone else in as this could open them up to the possibility of experiencing this unbearable pain again. A pain which they were not able to hold conscious awareness of that created drives unknown to the client. The client expressed their pain in behaviours without awareness that caused them to experience rejection from others creating more distress and protective behaviours. Thus, their unconscious drives created a cycle of rejection and a disorganised attachment model. With attachment patterns creating a blueprint of what to expect from others, it made a great deal of sense that the client would expect all adults to treat them similarly and for them to react against my approach of trying to understand them. It made sense that they would be motivated by unconscious drives to try to control the narrative that would repeat the cycle.

Bringing in a neurobiological, trauma-informed perspective, the brain likes what it knows. Safety in the brain is built on familiarity even when what is familiar hurts us. Our brains like to build patterns to help us make sense of the world and when a new experience comes along which disrupts these patterns, it will often set off the stress response. Out of our window of tolerance we go and up come one of the stress responses: fight, flight, hyper/hypo freeze, attach, fawn/appease, or submit/collapse. For this client, their fight response was activated which aims to create distance from the stressor. The client's loss was so significant and traumatic for them, the idea of connecting like this again was far too vulnerable for them to cope with. Their fight response had successfully ensured they were protected against experiencing the pain of their loss again by making sure others did not want to be around them. Wanting to connect with me at this stage would have made no logical sense as it would have meant the client's memory systems and nervous system were not operating to protect them, and the brain's primary goal of safety was not being met.

This experience taught me just how much empathy can hurt and just how triggering therapists can be. Therapists are taught to try to build a positive therapeutic connection with their clients. We are taught to offer attunement, acceptance, validation, holding, empathy, compassion, create safe spaces, repair ruptures, and so on. We are taught to challenge and explore alongside the client to help them make sense of their experiences. We are taught all this to build a model of secure attachment for our clients so that they can experience relational healing. The challenge in having these skills is the paradox this can create: the thing that promotes healing can be very the thing that is perceived by the client to be threatening.

Feeling seen, truly being seen, and being offered all that therapists are taught to offer, can and will leave many of our clients feeling unsafe. For clients where this feels unfamiliar, they may feel exposed and vulnerable. The therapeutic relationship can bring up all the loss of what they have not received from others. It can trigger memories of those who pretended to offer these relational qualities only to use them against the client, manipulate and hurt them. It can activate the client's shame and a lack of self-worth. It can even cause our client's immense pain to be offered these relationship skills. Thus, therapists can inadvertently be triggering and so it is to be expected that the client's defences will be activated to protect them, even the defences that will lead to directly attacking the therapist.

Three key takeaways from this experience:

1. **Empathy can be triggering**: Understanding and offering empathy can sometimes make clients feel exposed and vulnerable, particularly if their past experiences have conditioned them to view such interactions as threatening.

2. **Importance of trauma-informed practice**: Developing a deeper understanding of trauma and its impact on clients is crucial. This includes knowledge of the nervous system, stress responses, and the role of attachment patterns in client behaviour.

3. **Navigating client defences**: Recognising that client defences, even when expressed through hostility or rejection, are mechanisms for self-protection. Building a therapeutic relationship requires patience, consistency, and a non-reactive stance.

How did this experience help you improve your practice?

This experience highlighted the necessity of integrating trauma-informed approaches into therapeutic practice. It underscored the importance of understanding the neurobiological underpinnings of client behaviours and responses, leading to a more compassionate and effective approach to therapy. Additionally, it reinforced the value of flexibility and creativity in therapeutic interventions, such as using art to facilitate connection and healing.

How did clinical supervision support you through the experience? Did you access any additional supports?

Supervision was critical in providing guidance and reassurance, especially when dealing with challenging and unsettling client behaviours. It offered a space to process feelings of discomfort and confusion, gain new perspectives, and receive validation and support. Additionally, seeking out further training and education in trauma-informed practice and understanding the neurobiological aspects of trauma was essential. This ongoing professional development was supported by both formal supervision and informal peer consultations.

What insights have you gained from being curious about the experience and from the process of self-reflection?

Through self-reflection and curiosity, the insight gained was that client behaviours often serve as protective mechanisms rooted in past trauma. Understanding this can shift the therapeutic focus from the behaviour itself to the underlying pain and fear driving it. This perspective fosters greater empathy and patience, allowing for a more compassionate and effective therapeutic approach. Additionally, recognising the importance of maintaining one's own emotional regulation and self-care as a therapist was a significant insight, ensuring sustained capacity to support clients effectively.

What guidance and learning would you offer other professionals?

- **Embrace trauma-informed practice**: Continuously educate yourself on trauma and its effects on the brain and behaviour. Understanding these principles can transform your approach and enhance therapeutic outcomes.
- **Value supervision and peer support**: Regular supervision is invaluable for processing challenging cases, gaining new perspectives, and ensuring professional and personal growth. Engage in peer support networks for additional perspectives and emotional support.
- **Patience and non-reactivity**: Building trust and safety in the therapeutic relationship takes time, especially with clients who have experienced significant trauma Stay patient, consistent, and non-reactive in the face of challenging behaviours.
- **Use creative interventions**: Be open to using various therapeutic tools and approaches, such as art, to facilitate

connection and healing. Flexibility can help meet clients where they are and support their unique pathways to healing.

- **Self-care and emotional regulation**: Prioritise your own well-being and emotional regulation. Taking care of yourself ensures you can continue to provide the best support for your clients.

CHAPTER THIRTEEN

When Therapy Goes Awry: The Importance of Appropriate Referrals

Audrey Leckie MBACP

I am a therapeutic counsellor who has been studying and practising various models of therapy and support for roughly 20 years. I trained in a holistic setting where a broad consideration for individuality was paramount. Most likely because of this, I utilise an integrated model combining Cognitive Behavioural Therapy (CBT), person-centred, and psychodynamic counselling with my clients. For the past five years, I have worked for an independent charity working exclusively with survivors of historic Childhood Sexual Abuse (CSA), working mainly on a short-term basis with clients who have decided that they are ready to process and progress from their trauma.

I originally trained as a hairdresser. From 14 years old I worked in my local salon watching the physical and emotional transformations of the women who passed through those chairs. I noticed that I was an excellent empathetic listener, and that amazing changes could occur in a situation where a recognised safe space and explicit trust came together in the clearly defined relationship of client-hairdresser. This realisation, compounded with my innate desire to help and do more within my local community, inspired me to become a therapist.

A therapy session gone awry

Working for a charity, most of my clients are referred onto my caseload through word of mouth through the community or by health professionals familiar with our work. The positives of this design heavily outweigh the drawbacks, but in the instance I am about to share with you the drawbacks became potentially dangerous, despite the well-meaning nature of its origins.

On a Friday, I don't work from my usual office, with my usual staff or with my subconscious usual safeguards. Instead, I work on an outreach programme based in a doctor's office, allowing me to meet clients in a more convenient space. I work at the end of a long hallway of various treatment rooms with doctors, nurses and link workers occupying the rest. On this particular Friday afternoon, I was scheduled to meet with a new client referred by a local caseworker external to our organisation. So, I diligently prepared my paperwork and my office space and waited for their arrival. From the moment they arrived in my room, I realised we were not the right service to support this individual, and this individual was very likely suffering from unsupported paranoid schizophrenia and this individual did not care for my safety.

As they came into my room, I invited them to sit and share why they had met with me that day. They immediately started displaying erratic behaviour, curling in on themselves, throwing their arms wide with abandon, lunging forward into my space and espousing radical delusions. These delusions were built around the belief that the police, doctors, teachers, and other professions with a perceived position of power over the general community were all participating in a ring of organised, systemic child abuse and sacrifice. The individual shared that now they were speaking out, they would be targeted and silenced.

As they shared these delusions with me, they continued to lunge into my personal space, raising their voice and swearing at me and taking no regard for my protests and requests for them to maintain their own space.

I felt, for the first time in 20 years, unsafe.

Identifying factors contributing to challenges.

This scheduled therapy session and introduction had not gone to plan, and I asked the client to leave my room. This is something I had never done before in my 20 years of practice. I explained I could not work with them as they were refusing to observe my reasonable boundaries; they were refusing to treat me with basic respect and were not co-operating with any of my requests. I explained the service I was there to offer would not be suitable support for the level of help and guidance that would be necessary and safe for them, and I signposted them to where they could find this support. I confirmed I would willingly refer them on to speed the process along.

In this situation, the main dynamic factors which prevented success were the service offered was not adequate for the individual and could not meet their needs and the individual at that moment in time did not have a sound psychological thread to engage with, as well as the lack of defined roles to build trust from. The combination of these three factors would have meant that to continue the session would have been unethical, and inappropriate for both the client and me as the practitioner.

Approaching ethical considerations

For me, navigating ethical considerations can only be done with honesty and trust. In this situation, the ethical considerations were, was this safe - for the client and me - and was this appropriate? To assess this, I had to view the situation as it was in reality, reflect honestly and trust my experience to make a rational call.

The relationship between client and therapist is nothing without defined boundaries, trust and honest open dialogue, as without these elements, the therapist cannot commit to their duty of care, and the client cannot be afforded a safe environment to explore and build progress in the manner that they desire, thus making the situation unethical.

Impact of therapist-client relationship dynamics

In this situation, where a therapy session did not go to plan and did not go well at all - how has the relationship dynamic between the client and therapist changed? In this situation, I went from being an experienced professional to someone afraid and intimidated. The client went from being someone ready to speak out about their reality to being someone who had been disappointed by the service offered. This dynamic shift prevented progress and inhibited us from building a productive relationship which in turn stopped the therapy process entirely.

I cannot speak confidently on how the client might have felt in this instance as I am not in a qualified enough position to diagnose their condition. However, I can speculate through my experience that I will, to them, be another professional who has failed them, who has perhaps deceived them or stopped them accessing the support that they so clearly need, and I can only hope that this interaction will not prevent them from following up and accessing the appropriate support - but that is out of my control.

Addressing power imbalances

In this situation, it was not appropriate to resume the relationship, nor would the client have been capable of reflecting on the interaction with me so I cannot walk you through addressing a power imbalance in the context of this incident, so instead I provide my formula for re-establishing balance and trust within a therapeutic relationship for instances where it is appropriate.

Honestly check in with your client: Were the expectations and goals set at the start of your relationship realistic - and are they still relevant?

Do both parties think the relationship is progressing towards these goals in a supported (and professional) manner?

Can the client identify the issue that is causing feelings of discomfort/mistrust? And do they feel disempowered?

What does disempowerment/discomfort/mistrust mean to them?

In terms of short-term therapy, assessing if it is the right time for them to be undertaking therapy and consistently reviewing progress. Noting there may be consistent positive movement until they hit a block where they must then be invited to reflect and subsequently make an informed decision.

When I feel resistance from the client, at whatever point of their journey, I first name the resistance, and then explore it. The conversation usually looks something like this;

"It feels to me like you are resisting X part of therapy, can we explore what resistance is and what it means and feels like to you?"

From here, an honest and open dialogue can be maintained with the client retaining their power and autonomy while you, the therapist, maintain the boundaries and education of the therapy session.

This honest reflection with the client on how the journey has been to date is an opportunity to seek clarification and revisit the expectations and ground rules of the relationship, should the client wish to proceed at that point.

Three key takeaways from this experience:

- **Understanding the importance of safety and boundaries**: Ensuring both the client's and therapist's safety is paramount, and clearly defined boundaries are essential for establishing trust and maintaining a productive therapeutic relationship. In this situation, the lack of appropriate boundaries and the client's behaviour created an unsafe environment, highlighting the critical need for clear and enforceable boundaries in therapy.

- **Recognising the limitations of services**: It's important to recognise when a service or therapeutic approach may not be suitable for a client's needs. In this case, the client required a different level of support than what could be provided, demonstrating the necessity of appropriate referrals and understanding the limitations of one's practice.

- **Ethical decision-making in challenging situations**: Ethical considerations must guide therapeutic practice, especially in challenging situations. This experience reinforced the need for honesty, trust, and the ability to make difficult decisions to protect both the client's and therapist's well-being. However experienced the therapist is, there are always new firsts.

How did this experience help you improve your practice?

This experience helped me recognise the importance of assessing a client's needs early in the therapeutic relationship and being willing to make difficult decisions when those needs cannot be met within the scope of my practice. It reinforced the necessity of setting and maintaining clear boundaries, particularly in situations where safety is at risk. I also gained a deeper understanding of the ethical responsibilities involved in deciding when to end a session or refer a client to a more appropriate service.

How did clinical supervision support you through the experience? Did you access any additional supports?

Supervision was essential in helping me process this challenging experience. My supervisor provided a safe space to explore my feelings of fear and uncertainty, helping me to reflect on the ethical considerations and to reinforce the importance of boundaries in therapy. Additionally, I accessed peer support, where I discussed the situation with colleagues who had faced similar challenges, which helped me to feel less isolated and to gain new perspectives on handling such situations in the future.

What insights have you gained from being curious about the experience and from the process of self-reflection?

Through self-reflection, I gained insight into the importance of trusting my instincts when I feel unsafe or when the therapeutic environment becomes unmanageable. I learnt the value of being honest with myself and the client about the limitations of the service I can provide. This experience also highlighted the need to regularly reassess client needs and expectations, ensuring the therapeutic relationship remains appropriate and beneficial for both parties. There is always a first time.

What guidance and learning would you offer other professionals?

- **Prioritise safety and boundaries**: Always prioritise safety for both yourself and your clients. Clearly define and enforce boundaries from the outset of the therapeutic relationship.
- **Assess and recognise service limitations**: Be honest about the limitations of the services you can offer, and don't hesitate to refer clients to more appropriate support when necessary.
- **Engage in regular supervision and reflection**: Utilise supervision to process challenging experiences and to ensure that ethical considerations are at the forefront of your practice. Regular self-reflection and peer support can provide additional perspectives and help in navigating difficult situations.
- **Maintain open dialogue with clients**: When encountering resistance or challenges in the therapeutic relationship, engage in honest and open dialogue with clients to explore their feelings and concerns, ensuring that their autonomy and the integrity of the therapeutic process are maintained.

Acknowledgement

I would like to extend my deepest gratitude to my daughter, Lauren, who played an invaluable role in the creation of this chapter. As my scribe and grammar guide, Lauren's keen eye and dedication helped me bring my ideas to life, ensuring that my thoughts were communicated clearly and effectively. Her support was especially crucial given my challenges with processing dyslexia. Thank you, Lauren, for your patience, skill, and unwavering belief in me. This work would not have been possible without you.

CHAPTER FOURTEEN

A Reflection of the Role of Supervision in Counselling and Psychotherapy: A Journey Through 13 Therapist Experiences

By Satinder Panesar

In the world of counselling and psychotherapy, supervision is not just a professional requirement but a critical tool for maintaining ethical practice, ensuring well-being, and fostering personal and professional growth. The 13 chapters in this book delve deeply into the diverse scenarios where counsellors, psychotherapists, and counselling psychologists found themselves seeking supervision, often under complex and challenging circumstances. These narratives highlight the essential role of supervision in providing support, guidance, and reflection, allowing practitioners to navigate their work ethically and effectively.

Supervision as a lifeline in ethical dilemmas

One of the most prevalent reasons for seeking supervision, as explored in several chapters, is the need to navigate ethical dilemmas. Whether it's balancing the confidentiality of a client with potential harm, managing dual relationships, or grappling with boundaries, these stories illustrate how supervision acts as a safe space where practitioners can discuss these difficult decisions without fear of judgement. Supervision not only helps the therapist explore the ethical dimensions of their work but also provides clarity on the application of ethical frameworks.

Personal well-being and the role of supervision

Another recurring theme is the use of supervision to safeguard the mental and emotional well-being of the therapists. Counselling and psychotherapy are emotionally demanding professions, and without proper support, therapists can experience burnout, compassion fatigue and vicarious trauma. The chapters provide real-life examples where therapists sought supervision after feeling overwhelmed by their client's issues, struggling with feelings of inadequacy, or dealing with personal crises that affected their ability to remain present for their clients.

Supervision in complex client scenarios

Supervision is also vital when therapists encounter complex or challenging client scenarios that require additional insight or expertise. The chapters explore situations where practitioners faced difficulties with transference, countertransference, and ruptures in the therapeutic relationship. In these instances, supervision provided a space for the therapist to explore these dynamics, understand their own reactions, and adjust their therapeutic approach.

Supervision for professional development

Beyond addressing immediate concerns, the chapters also emphasise the role of supervision in ongoing professional development. Supervision is not only about addressing problems but also about fostering growth, enhancing skills, and exploring new theoretical approaches. Several chapters highlight how practitioners used supervision as a space for reflection on their practice, identifying areas for improvement, and gaining new insights into their work.

A collaborative and safe space

The stories in these chapters underscore the collaborative nature of supervision. The relationship between supervisor and supervisee is built on trust, respect, and a shared commitment to the therapist's development and the well-being of their clients. Supervision offers a non-judgemental space where therapists can bring their uncertainties, vulnerabilities, and mistakes without fear of criticism. This environment fosters a culture of continuous learning, where mistakes are viewed as opportunities for growth, and challenges are approached with curiosity and openness.

In conclusion, the 13 chapters provide a rich and nuanced exploration of how supervision supports the work of counsellors, psychotherapists, and counselling psychologists. Whether facing ethical dilemmas, personal struggles, complex client dynamics, or simply seeking professional growth, supervision emerges as an essential tool that ensures both the well-being of the practitioner, and the quality of care provided to clients. By offering support, guidance, and reflection, supervision safeguards the integrity and effectiveness of the therapeutic process, making it a fundamental pillar of ethical and sustainable practice.

CHAPTER FIFTEEN

Choosing the Right Supervisor: The Importance of the Supervisory Relationship

Choosing the right clinical supervisor is a pivotal decision for counsellors and psychotherapists. The right supervisor can significantly enhance your professional growth, support your practice, and ensure the delivery of high-quality care to your clients. This comprehensive guide explores the essential factors to consider when selecting a clinical supervisor, including qualifications, compatibility, supervision style, ethical standards, commitment to development, feedback mechanisms, accessibility, cultural competence, reputation, and self-reflection.

Clinical supervision is a cornerstone of effective therapeutic practice, providing counsellors and psychotherapists with guidance, support, and professional development opportunities. Given its importance, finding a suitable supervisor is crucial. The right supervisor not only facilitates your growth as a therapist but also enhances the therapeutic outcomes for your clients.

Qualifications and experience
Credentials
- Ensure the supervisor holds the necessary qualifications and certifications relevant to your field. They should have an appropriate level of education and experience.
- Check for membership in professional organisations, such as the British Association for Counselling and Psychotherapy (BACP), National Counselling & Psychotherapy Society (NCPS) or Counselling & Psychotherapy in Scotland (COSCA).

Clinical experience

- The supervisor should have substantial experience in clinical practice, particularly in the areas where you seek to develop your expertise. This includes experience with specific client populations, therapeutic approaches, and presenting issues.
- Look for a supervisor who has a proven track record of effective supervision. Experience as a supervisor, rather than just as a clinician, is crucial because supervising requires different skills.

Compatibility and rapport

Personal compatibility

- Compatibility in personality and values is essential. You should feel comfortable, respected, and understood by your supervisor. A strong interpersonal fit enhances the supervisory relationship and fosters open communication.
- Consider scheduling an initial meeting or consultation to assess whether you connect well with the potential supervisor.

Communication style

- The supervisor's communication style should align with your preferences. They should be able to provide feedback in a way that you find constructive and supportive.
- Effective supervisors are good listeners, empathetic, and able to communicate clearly and effectively.

Supervision style and approach

Supervision models

- Understand the theoretical orientation and supervision model employed by the supervisor. Common models include developmental, integrative, reflective, and systemic supervision.
- Ensure that the supervisor's approach aligns with your own therapeutic orientation or the one you wish to develop. For example, if you practice cognitive-behavioural therapy, a supervisor with expertise in that area would be beneficial.

- Ask what Clinical Supervision model they follow i.e. Seven Eyed Model of Supervision

Flexibility

- A supervisor should be flexible and adaptable, tailoring their approach to meet your developmental needs. They should be able to provide structured guidance when necessary and encourage independent thinking as you gain confidence and experience.

Ethical and professional standards
Adherence to ethics

- The supervisor should adhere to high ethical standards and be well-versed in the ethical guidelines. They should model ethical behaviour and help you navigate ethical dilemmas.
- Confirm the supervisor has a clear understanding of confidentiality, professional boundaries, and other critical ethical issues in therapy.

Boundaries

- Effective supervisors maintain clear professional boundaries and foster a respectful, professional relationship. This helps in creating a safe and productive environment for supervision.

Commitment to your development
Supportive environment

- The supervisor should create a supportive environment where you feel safe to discuss your cases and reflect on your practice. This includes being approachable and empathetic.
- They should offer a balance of support and challenge, providing guidance while encouraging you to grow and develop as a therapist.

Focus on growth

- A supervisor who is genuinely interested in your professional growth will provide opportunities for you to develop your skills and knowledge. They should help you set clear, achievable goals and support your progress over time.
- Look for a supervisor who encourages continuous learning and professional development, such as attending workshops, conferences, and other training opportunities.

Feedback and evaluation

Constructive feedback

- The supervisor should provide regular, constructive feedback that helps you improve your practice. They should be honest yet supportive in their feedback.
- Effective feedback should be specific, actionable, and focused on both strengths and areas for improvement.

Goal setting

- A supervisor works with you to set clear, achievable goals for your professional development. These goals should be aligned with your career aspirations and areas of interest.
- Regularly reviewing and adjusting these goals ensures that you are continually progressing and addressing new challenges as they arise.

Accessibility and availability

Regular meetings

- Ensure the supervisor is available for regular supervision sessions. The frequency and duration of these sessions should meet your needs and be agreed upon in advance.
- Regular supervision is crucial for ongoing professional development and support and is a requirement – number of hours required will be dependent on your professional registering body.

Responsive

- The supervisor should be responsive to your queries and concerns, providing timely feedback and support. This is particularly important in urgent or complex/risk cases where immediate guidance may be necessary.

Cultural competence

Cultural awareness

- The supervisor should be culturally competent, understanding and respecting your cultural background and that of your clients. They should be able to address issues related to diversity and inclusion in therapy.
- Look for a supervisor who has experience working with diverse populations and is committed to ongoing learning in this area.

Inclusivity

- They should foster an inclusive environment where diversity is valued and discussed openly. This includes being aware of and addressing any potential biases or blind spots in their supervision.

Reputation and references

Professional reputation

- Look for a supervisor with a strong professional reputation. This can be assessed through recommendations from colleagues, professional networks, and reviews.
- A supervisor with a good reputation is likely to have a history of effective supervision and satisfied supervisees.

References

- Consider asking for references or testimonials from other supervisees who have worked with the supervisor. This can provide valuable insights into the supervisor's effectiveness, style, and approach.

- Speaking directly with former supervisees can give you a better sense of what to expect from the supervisory relationship.

Self-reflection and feedback

Reflect on sessions

- After supervision sessions, reflect on how you feel about the interaction. Do you leave feeling supported, challenged, and motivated to improve? Your emotional and professional reactions are critical indicators of the suitability of the supervisor.
- Pay attention to whether the supervisor respects your input and encourages your growth, or if you feel stifled or unsupported.

Seek feedback

- Don't hesitate to seek feedback from peers or mentors about your supervisory relationship. Sometimes an external perspective can be very enlightening.
- Regularly evaluate the supervisory relationship to ensure it continues to meet your needs. If necessary, be prepared to discuss any concerns with your supervisor or seek a new supervisor if the relationship is not beneficial.

Conclusion

Choosing the right clinical supervisor is a critical decision that can significantly impact your professional development and the quality of care you provide. By carefully considering factors such as qualifications, compatibility, supervision style, ethical standards, commitment to development, feedback mechanisms, accessibility, cultural competence, reputation, and self-reflection, you can make an informed choice. The right supervisor will not only support your growth as a therapist but also enhance the therapeutic outcomes for your clients. Remember, the supervisory relationship is dynamic and should evolve to meet your needs as you grow in your practice. Prioritising your professional development and well-being in this process is essential for a successful and fulfilling career in counselling and psychotherapy.

"If you don't hop, skip and jump to clinical supervision –
reflect on why?"
Satinder Panesar

Chapter Sixteen

The Importance of Clinical Supervision and Peer Support for Counsellors & Psychotherapists

Clinical supervision and peer support are vital components of professional practice for counsellors and psychotherapists. They serve as foundational pillars that enhance the quality of client care, foster professional development, and uphold ethical standards.

Counselling and psychotherapy are demanding professions that require continuous personal and professional growth. The complexities of human behaviour and emotional well-being necessitate a robust support system for practitioners. Clinical supervision and peer support are integral to this system, providing a structured and collaborative environment for therapists to reflect, learn, and develop their practice.

Clinical supervision
Definition and purpose
Clinical supervision is a formal process wherein an experienced therapist (supervisor) provides guidance, support, and feedback to another therapist (supervisee). The primary purposes of clinical supervision are:

- **Professional development:** Enhancing the supervisee's clinical skills, theoretical knowledge, and self-awareness.
- **Quality of client care:** Ensuring the effectiveness and ethical integrity of the therapeutic services provided to clients.
- **Emotional support:** Offering a safe space for therapists to process their own emotional responses and experiences.

Roles and functions
- **Educational role:** Supervisors impart knowledge and skills, helping supervisees integrate theoretical understanding with practical application. They provide insights into various

therapeutic approaches and techniques, fostering a deeper comprehension of client dynamics.

- **Supportive role:** Supervisors offer emotional and psychological support, helping supervisees manage the stresses and emotional demands of their work. This support is crucial in preventing burnout and promoting resilience.

- **Evaluative role:** Supervisors assess the supervisee's performance, providing constructive feedback and identifying areas for improvement. This evaluative function ensures that the supervisee's practice meets professional standards.

Models of clinical supervision

Several models guide the practice of clinical supervision, each with unique approaches:

- **Developmental models:** These models view supervision as a process of professional growth, with supervisees progressing through various stages of competence. Supervisors adapt their approach based on the supervisee's developmental stage, providing more structure and guidance to beginners and more autonomy to experienced therapists.

- **Integrative models:** Integrative supervision incorporates multiple theoretical orientations, allowing supervisors to tailor their approach to the specific needs of the supervisee and their clients. This model emphasises flexibility and adaptability.

- **Reflective models:** Reflective supervision focuses on fostering self-awareness and critical thinking. Supervisors encourage supervisees to reflect on their practice, explore their reactions, and understand the therapeutic process more deeply.

- **Systemic models:** Systemic supervision considers the broader context in which therapy occurs, including family, social, and organisational systems. It emphasises understanding the interactions between these systems and their impact on the therapeutic process.

Benefits of clinical supervision

- **Enhanced clinical skills:** Supervision provides a platform for continuous learning and skill development. Supervisors share their expertise, helping supervisees refine their therapeutic techniques and strategies.
- **Improved client outcomes:** By ensuring high-quality, ethical practice, supervision directly contributes to better client outcomes. Supervisors offer alternative perspectives and strategies that enhance the effectiveness of therapy.
- **Professional growth:** Supervision fosters ongoing professional development, keeping therapists updated with the latest research, theories, and best practices. It encourages a culture of lifelong learning.
- **Emotional resilience:** The supportive nature of supervision helps therapists manage the emotional toll of their work, reducing the risk of burnout and promoting well-being.
- **Ethical practice:** Supervisors guide supervisees through ethical dilemmas, ensuring adherence to professional standards and
- safeguarding client welfare.

Peer support

Definition and purpose

Peer support involves informal, collaborative interactions between therapists of similar levels of experience. It aims to provide mutual support, share knowledge, and foster a sense of community among practitioners. Unlike clinical supervision, peer support is typically non-hierarchical and emphasises reciprocal relationships.

Roles and functions

- **Emotional support:** Peer support offers a safe space for therapists to share their experiences, challenges, and successes with colleagues who understand their professional context. This mutual support is essential for emotional well-being.
- **Professional development:** Peers share knowledge,

resources, and insights, enhancing each other's professional growth. They provide feedback and suggestions based on their experiences and perspectives.

- **Collaboration and networking:** Peer support fosters a collaborative environment where therapists can network, exchange ideas, and develop professional relationships. This networking can lead to opportunities for further development and collaboration.

Forms of peer support

- **Peer supervision groups:** These groups consist of therapists who meet regularly to discuss cases, share experiences, and provide mutual support and feedback. Peer supervision groups are a valuable resource for continuous learning and support.
- **Informal peer meetings:** Informal meetings or discussions with colleagues provide opportunities for spontaneous support and knowledge sharing. These interactions can occur in various settings, such as over coffee or during breaks at conferences.
- **Online forums and communities:** Online platforms offer opportunities for therapists to connect with peers, share resources, and seek advice. These forums can be particularly beneficial for those in remote areas or with limited access to local peer support.

Benefits of peer support

- **Reduced Isolation:** Peer support helps therapists feel less isolated, providing a sense of community and belonging. This is particularly important for those in private practice or rural areas.
- **Shared Learning:** Peers can learn from each other's experiences, gaining new perspectives and insights. This shared learning enhances professional competence and confidence.
- **Increased Resilience:** Mutual support helps therapists manage stress and build resilience. Sharing experiences and challenges with peers can provide comfort and validation, reducing the risk of burnout.

- **Professional Identity:** Peer support reinforces a sense of professional identity and commitment. It encourages therapists to stay engaged with their profession and adhere to its values and standards.

Integration of clinical supervision and peer support

Integrating clinical supervision and peer support provides a comprehensive support system for therapists. Each has distinct but complementary roles, and together they offer a holistic approach to professional development and well-being.

- **Balanced support:** Combining structured supervision with informal peer support ensures that therapists receive both expert guidance and mutual support. This balance addresses different aspects of professional growth and emotional well-being.
- **Diverse perspectives:** Supervisors provide expert insights and feedback, while peers offer diverse perspectives and practical advice. This diversity enriches the learning experience and enhances problem-solving.
- **Continuous learning:** Clinical supervision offers formal, ongoing learning opportunities, while peer support provides informal, continuous knowledge sharing. Together, they foster a culture of lifelong learning and development.
- **Comprehensive well-being:** The emotional support provided by both supervisors and peers helps therapists maintain their well-being and resilience. This comprehensive support system addresses the multifaceted challenges of therapeutic work.

Challenges and considerations

While clinical supervision and peer support offer numerous benefits, they also present certain challenges:

- **Power dynamics:** The hierarchical nature of supervision can create power imbalances. Supervisors must be mindful of maintaining a supportive and respectful relationship with supervisees.

- **Time constraints:** Finding time for regular supervision and peer support meetings can be challenging, especially for therapists with busy schedules. Prioritising these activities is crucial for long-term well-being and professional growth.
- **Access to quality supervision:** Not all therapists have access to high-quality supervision, particularly in rural or underserved areas. Online supervision and peer support networks can help bridge this gap.
- **Maintaining boundaries:** Balancing professional and personal boundaries in peer support relationships is essential to ensure mutual respect and effectiveness.
- **Diversity and inclusion:** Supervisors and peer groups must be culturally competent and inclusive, respecting the diverse backgrounds and experiences of all members.

Conclusion

Clinical supervision and peer support are indispensable elements of professional practice for counsellors and psychotherapists. They provide the necessary framework for continuous learning, ethical practice, and emotional resilience. By integrating structured supervision with informal peer support, therapists can enhance their skills, improve client outcomes, and maintain their well-being. Despite the challenges, the benefits of these support systems make them essential for fostering a thriving, competent, and ethical professional community. As the field of counselling and psychotherapy continues to evolve, the importance of clinical supervision and peer support will remain paramount in ensuring the highest standards of care and professional excellence.

CHAPTER SEVENTEEN

The Importance of Adapting Learning from Mistakes and Improving Practice for Counsellors & Psychotherapists

Introduction

The field of counselling and psychotherapy is inherently complex, requiring practitioners to navigate the intricacies of human behaviour and emotional well-being. Mistakes, while often uncomfortable, are inevitable and can serve as valuable learning opportunities. Adapting and learning from these mistakes is crucial for professional growth, the enhancement of therapeutic practice, and the overall effectiveness of client care. This chapter explores the importance of embracing mistakes, the process of learning from them, and strategies for continuous improvement.

Counsellors and psychotherapists operate in a dynamic and often unpredictable environment. Given the variability of human experience and the uniqueness of each client, errors and setbacks are a natural part of practice. The ability to recognise, learn from, and adapt to these mistakes is essential for personal and professional development. By fostering a mindset of continuous improvement, therapists can enhance their skills, improve client outcomes, and maintain ethical standards.

The nature of mistakes in therapy
Understanding mistakes

Mistakes in therapy can take various forms, including clinical errors, ethical lapses, miscommunications, and personal oversights. Examples include not diagnosing, inappropriate interventions, boundary violations, or failure to adequately address a client's needs. Understanding the nature of these mistakes is the first step towards addressing and learning from them.

Impact on clients and therapists

Mistakes can have significant consequences for both clients and therapists. For clients, errors can result in unmet needs, prolonged distress, or a loss of trust in the therapeutic process. For therapists, mistakes can lead to feelings of guilt, shame, and self-doubt, potentially impacting their confidence and effectiveness. Recognising the impact of mistakes underscores the importance of addressing them constructively.

The importance of adapting and learning from mistakes
Professional growth

- **Self-awareness:** Mistakes offer an opportunity for self-reflection and increased self-awareness. By examining errors, therapists can gain insights into their blind spots, biases, and areas needing improvement. This self-awareness is fundamental to personal and professional growth.
- **Skill enhancement:** Learning from mistakes allows therapists to refine their clinical skills and therapeutic techniques. Understanding what went wrong and why can lead to more effective interventions and better client outcomes in the future.

Improved client outcomes

- **Enhanced therapeutic effectiveness:** By addressing and correcting mistakes, therapists can improve the quality of care they provide. This leads to more effective therapeutic relationships and better client outcomes.
- **Building trust:** Clients are more likely to trust therapists who acknowledge their mistakes and take steps to rectify them. This transparency and commitment to improvement can strengthen the therapeutic alliance and foster a more collaborative relationship.

Ethical Practice

- Maintaining standards: Ethical practice requires a commitment to continuous learning and improvement. By learning from mistakes, therapists uphold the ethical standards of their profession, ensuring that they provide the best possible care to their clients

- **Preventing reoccurrence:** Addressing mistakes helps prevent their **reoccurrence**. By implementing changes based on past errors, therapists can avoid making the same mistakes in the future, thereby safeguarding their clients' well-being.

Strategies for adapting and learning from mistakes

Reflective practice

- **Regular reflection:** Engage in regular reflection on your practice. This can be done through journalling, supervision, or peer discussions. Reflective practice helps identify areas for improvement and develop strategies for addressing mistakes.

- **Case reviews:** Review challenging cases to understand what went wrong and why. Discuss these cases in supervision or with peers to gain different perspectives and insights.

Supervision and consultation

- **Utilise supervision:** Regular supervision provides a safe space to discuss mistakes, seek feedback, and develop strategies for improvement. Supervisors can offer valuable guidance and support, helping therapists learn from their errors.

- **Seek consultation:** In addition to supervision, consult with colleagues or experts when faced with difficult cases or ethical dilemmas. Consultation can provide new insights and alternative approaches, enhancing your practice.

Continuing education

- **Professional development:** Engage in continuing education and professional development opportunities. Attend workshops, conferences, and training sessions to stay updated with the latest research, techniques, and best practices in the field.

- **Specialised training:** Pursue specialised training in areas where you feel less confident or have made mistakes. This targeted learning can help address specific gaps in your knowledge and skills.

Feedback Mechanisms

- **Client feedback:** Encourage clients to provide feedback on their experience. This can help identify areas for improvement and provide valuable insights into your practice.
- **Peer feedback:** Engage in peer supervision or peer support groups where you can give and receive feedback. Peer feedback can offer different perspectives and help identify blind spots.

Self-care and resilience

- **Practice self-care:** Managing the emotional impact of mistakes requires effective self-care. Engage in activities that promote your well-being, such as exercise, hobbies, and mindfulness practices.
- **Build resilience:** Develop resilience by fostering a growth mindset and viewing mistakes as opportunities for learning Building resilience helps manage stress and maintain a positive outlook.

Ethical decision-making

- **Ethical frameworks:** Familiarise yourself with ethical frameworks and guidelines in your profession. Use these frameworks to guide your practice and decision-making.
- **Ethical reflection:** Reflect on ethical dilemmas and mistakes from an ethical perspective. Consider the implications of your actions and how you can uphold ethical standards in future situations.

Overcoming barriers to learning from mistakes

Addressing shame and guilt

- **Acknowledge emotions:** Recognise and acknowledge feelings of shame and guilt associated with mistakes. These emotions are natural but can hinder learning if not addressed.
- **Self-compassion:** Practice self-compassion and forgive yourself for mistakes. Understand that errors are part of the learning process and do not define your competence as a therapist.

Cultivating a growth mindset

- **Embrace learning:** Adopt a growth mindset that views mistakes as opportunities for learning and growth This mindset fosters resilience and a proactive approach to improvement.
- **Celebrate progress:** Celebrate your progress and successes, no matter how small. Acknowledging your growth helps build confidence and motivation to continue improving.

Creating a supportive environment

- **Supportive networks:** Surround yourself with supportive colleagues and mentors who encourage learning and growth. A supportive environment fosters open discussions about mistakes and promotes collective learning.
- **Organisational culture:** Advocate for an organisational culture that values continuous improvement and supports learning from mistakes. This culture should prioritise professional development and ethical practice.

Conclusion

Adapting, learning from mistakes, and improving practice are essential components of effective counselling and psychotherapy. Mistakes, while challenging, provide valuable opportunities for self-awareness, skill enhancement, and professional growth. By embracing reflective practice, supervision, continuing education, feedback mechanisms, self-care, and ethical decision-making, therapists can transform errors into learning experiences. Overcoming barriers to learning, such as shame and guilt, and cultivating a supportive environment further facilitate this process. Ultimately, the commitment to continuous improvement ensures that therapists provide the highest quality of care to their clients, fostering trust, ethical practice, and positive therapeutic outcomes.

WAYS OF WORKING WITH ME

Clinical consultancy

I offer tailored clinical consultancy services to support a wide range of needs in mental health and wellness.

- Collaborate on specialised projects in mental health and wellness.
- Provide expert guidance to develop clinical programs or workshops.
- Provide clinical consultation services for organisations.
- Partner with corporate companies to design and implement workplace wellness programs.

Supervision, reflective practice, and mentorship

Supporting other mental health professionals is a key aspect of my work.

- Offer clinical supervision for therapists and mental health practitioners.
- Provide reflective practice sessions and mentorship to focus on ethical practice, case management, and professional growth.
- Universities, Colleges, and Educational Institutions
- I Partner with educational institutions to support mental health within the student community
- Deliver guest lectures or training sessions such as Clinical Supervision or Mental Health topics for academic courses or faculty development.

Therapy

My therapy services are designed to meet the unique needs of individuals and groups.

- Offer individual therapy sessions to address personal challenges.
- Facilitate group therapy opportunities focused on shared experiences or themes.
- Please feel free to get in touch if you would like to discuss any of these services or explore other ways we might work together. I am always open to tailoring my expertise to meet your specific needs and objectives.

Download my Top 10 Tips for Being a Therapist here:

Satinder Panesar
www.satinderpanesar.com
itsallaboutyou@satinderpanesar.com

Connect With The Contributors

Annie Lee Garrigan
Ani de la Prida,
Association of Person-Centred Creative Arts
annieleegarrigan@protonmail.com

Alison Carter Counselling
www.alisoncartercounselling.com

Amrita Dash
https://www.bacp.co.uk/therapists/385688/amrita-dash/

Audrey Leckie MBACP
https://www.linkedin.com/in/audrey-leckie-mbacp-dip-a165946b/

Caroline O'Grady
caroline.ogrady@icloud.com

Debbie Bolton
debbie.bolton@yahoo.co.uk
www.psychologytoday.com

Dr M G Shippi
https://www.drmgshippi.com/about/

Lee Patterson
https://www.counselling-directory.org.uk/counsellors/
lee-paterson

Lizzy Pittock
Therapy With Lizzy
www.therapywithlizzy.com

Michelle McQuillan
michellemcquillancounselling.com

Ravind Jeawon
https://talktherapy.ie/talk-therapy-rathmines/therapist-
dublin-6w/

Ruth Daly
www.ruthdaly.co.uk

Steven Queen
Empathy Rooms
www.empathyrooms.com